Welcome to the 10th edition of Itchy. Wh

you're an Itchy virgin or an old flame, we

here to help you make the most of going

in Sheffield. We hope you enjoy yourselve

much as we have over the last 10 years..

IN-HOUSE TEAM

Editor: Mike Toller

Local editor: Joly Braime

Features editor: Alexi Duggins

Editorial and production assistants:
Clare Cullen, Alix Fox

Editorial assistants: Jon Lynes, Anton Tweedale

Editorial assistance: Iliana Dracou, Sam Shields,
Achmed Esser, Cory Burdette, Lily Gorlin,
Rozanne Gelbinovich, Maisie McCabe,
Julie Dyer, Jackie Fishman

Designers: Paul Jones, Sara Gramner

Design assistance: Katelyn Boller

Picture research: Tiago Genoveze,
Philip Kelly, Neha Bhargava, Katelyn Boller

Production consultant: Iain Leslie

National ad sales: Sue Ostler, Zee Ahmad

Local ad sales: Gemma Coldwell

Distribution: Efua Hagan

Financial controller: Sharon Watkins

Managing director: Ian Merricks

Publisher: Itchy Group

© 2008 Itchy Group

ISBN: 978-1-905705-37-5

SHEFFIELD TEAM

City editors: Kerrie Barnett & Emma Davis

Contributors: Leo Smith, Angus Hutchison,
Bryony Clare, Jordan Cullen, Kirsty Bowen,
Samuel Cutting, Emma Taylor, Amy Berman,
Richard Avery, Dame Amy

Photography: Marc Doris, Selma Yalazi Dawani,
Tim Ireland, Chris Grossmeier, Ross Williams,
Mario Alberto, Tiago Genoveze

Cover and feature illustrations: www.si-clark.co.uk

Itchy

Itchy Group
78 Liverpool Road, London, N1 0QD
Tel: 020 7288 9810
Fax: 020 7288 9815
E-mail: editor@itchymedia.co.uk
Web: www.itchycity.co.uk

Itchy Contents

Introduction 6

Welcome to Sheffield,
welcome to Itchy.
Here's the lowdown
on all the high life

Eat 11

Hungry? We know
where you can fill your
boots and bellies

Contents

ITCHY · 10TH · BIRTHDAY · ITCHY · 10TH

Introduction

Welcome to Sheffield

SHEFFIELD – CITY ON THE MOVE

Happy birthday to us, happy birthday to us, happy birthday dear u-us, happy birthday to us. We can hardly believe it's been 10 years since we first opened our pages to the sights and sounds of good ol' Sheffield, this Nirvana of the North. But don't worry, we're not quite ready for the knacker's yard just yet (and when we do get sent down, we're taking you with us). We're still brimming with excitement at all things Sheffield. And if you thought Sheffield was only about steel and unemployed strippers, perhaps Pulp and The Arctic Monkeys would beg to differ. And if you fear urban sprawl, did you know Sheff has more trees per person than any other city in Europe? Not to mention the Peak District. And for culture, there's the breathtakingly cutting-edge Sheffield Crucible Theatre, that also hosts the odd snooker match. So, let's all hold hands and take a deep breath as we plunge headlong into everything this great town has to offer.

10 years

Changes in Sheffield over the last ten years

BACK IN THE DARK AGES OF THE 20TH CENTURY SHEFFIELD COULD HAVE BEEN SEEN AS A PRETTY GLOOMY PLACE: A MASS OF GREY CONCRETE WITH THE MOOR AS ONE OF ITS MAIN SHOPPING ATTRACTIONS. NICE. COMPARED TO THE CULTURED CITIES OF LEEDS AND MANCHESTER NEARBY , SHEFFIELD SEEMED LIKE THE PLAIN JANE NEXT DOOR. HOWEVER, WITH THE 21ST CENTURY CAME THE ARRIVAL OF CRANES AND BULLDOZERS GALORE, AND SHEFFIELD FINALLY GREW UP AND TURNED INTO A BEAUTIFUL SWAN.

Of course the infamous *Full Monty* helped to plonk Sheffield on the map, and those cheeky Arctic Monkeys (and more recently Reverend and The Makers), are showing the music world that Sheffield is a force to be reckoned with. Like one of the randy pigeons littering its streets, the steel city is puffing out its chest and asserting its dominance over all competitors. Redevelopment projects galore have transformed the city centre, so it's all a lot easier on the eye. The train station, for instance, now welcomes you to the city with trickling waterfalls and lights, rather than making you want to run, screaming back inside for a train to rescue you from the depressing urban jungle of yesteryear. Accompanying this are the multiple-births of cosmopolitan bars and stylish watering holes, so you'll never get bored of choosing which place you want to buy your next mojito from.

However, be warned – for with the new trendy vibe that Sheffield is casting has come the arrival of the schmoozing poseurs whose sole aim is to be seen, particularly along the Ecclesall Road where super car after sports car lines the street. But as long as you're not the bitter and jealous type you might actually quite enjoy gawping at them, saying bloke things like, 'ooh look at the body on that' (the car that is, not the poseur). Okay, well maybe the poseur as well, but we guess it depends.

But of course these rich luvvies won't stand in the way of your appreciation for the great city of steel. Prospects galore ooze from its walls; jobs are on offer from businesses moving in; there's a choice of stylish bars and shops, a blinding music scene and eventually, those magical building men will make us one of the most beautiful cities in the land.

Introduction

Local Lingo

ORREIGHT THERE LOVE? LEMME 'AVE A NANKLE WIT' YOUR PUSH-IRON – ARE YOU OK? LET ME HAVE A GO AT FIXING YOUR BIKE. WHA THA GOT FOR THEE SNAP? – WHAT HAVE YOU FOR YOUR LUNCH? AH COUL' REELLY DO WIT' A MASH REET NAH, DUCK – I WOULD REALLY LIKE A CUP OF TEA RIGHT NOW. EE'S A BIT NESH, INNIT? T'AIN'T THAT PARKY – HE'S A BIT OF A WIMP WHEN IT COMES TO THE COLD ISN'T HE? IT ISN'T THAT COLD. NAHDEN, PUTWOODINTOYAL AND CUMMINSIDE – NOW THEN, CLOSE THE DOOR AND COME INSIDE. AYYUP LOVE, WHATCHA DOIN WITH THOSE BICKIES? PURRUMINEER – HANG ON A MINUTE, WHAT ARE YOU DOING WITH THOSE BISCUITS? PUT THEM IN HERE. AH DUNNO NOWT ABOUT IT, BURROUR LASS DOES – I KNOW NOTHING ABOUT IT, BUT MY WIFE DOES. AH LUKEDIT UP ON 'TINTERWEB AND IT'S GONNABE SYLIN DOWN ON'TCHOWZDI – I LOOKED IT UP ON THE WORLD WIDE WEB AND IT'S GOING TO BE RAINING REALLY HARD ON TUESDAY. EE'S MARDY COS EE'AS TO WORK NINE WHILE FIVE – HE'S IN A MISERABLE MOOD BECAUSE HE HAS TO WORK 9 UNTIL 5. EH?? AH FORT YOU SED GERROFF T' CAUSIE – PARDON? I THOUGHT YOU SAID GET OFF THE PAVEMENT.

Top five places to have your photo taken

Spearmint Rhino: Dress in a mac and trilby and don a fake moustache. Strike a pose to make it look as though you've been snapped leaving in disguise.

The train station: Drape yourself against one of the many waterfalls, Paris photo-shoot stylee. Have someone take continuity Polaroids of you alongside the real 'photographer' for extra photo shoot authenticity.

Winter Gardens: Get some khaki gear and an explorer's hat and snap a shot of you peering out between the tropical plants in a David Attenborough-esque way.

Next to a Sheffield tram: A pair of glasses taped together with a plaster, a woolly hat and notepad will have your parents believing you've taken up tram spotting – like every good, northerner should – when you write home to them.

Sheffield Ski Slope: Get an action shot of you doing a one-legged stunt down the slope. Save some film for the priceless shots you'll get of you screaming on a stretcher with a broken thigh.

Quirky facts

The Arts Tower, which is part of the University of Sheffield, has the largest surviving paternoster lifts in the UK. Ride it all the way over the top of the building if you're looking for a cheap thrill.

Sheffield United is the world's oldest football club. Formed in 1857 as a way of keeping a cricket club together through the winter season. Cricket was still played at Bramall lane until 1975.

As you're heading into Northern territory on entering Sheffield, it's no surprise that, on average, it's a whole 2°C lower in temperature than London. But it's not all cold news, as it's also nearly 2°C higher in temperature than Edinburgh.

George Orwell called Sheffield 'the ugliest town in the Old World'. Now it's the greenest city in the country and has more trees per person than any city in Europe. Ha, so much for Orwell.

Sheffield has its own Walk of Fame. Head to the town hall to look at plaques dedicated to Sean Bean, Jarvis Cocker, Def Leppard and Michael Palin.

Eat

Eat

Welcome to Eat

Your head's banging and your mouth tastes like a badger has done unspeakable things in it all night. To help feed the mother of all hangovers there's **Yankees (418 Ecclesall Road, 0114 268 0828)**. One meal there will have you refuelled and ready for your next drink. If you're feeling sturdier at the end of your weekend and the only thing you're craving is a good Sunday lunch then get yourself along to **The Showroom Café (7 Paternoster Row, 0114 249 5479)**. Not the most traditional of places to get a roast but it does a mean leg of lamb and its trimmings will have you ready for a well-deserved afternoon nap. If meat doesn't float your boat though **Las Iguanas (8–9 West One, Fitzwilliam Street, 0114 252 1010)** provides some solid, and delicious, vegetarian dishes. They've even made it easy to choose which Latin delights to devour by putting a handy little 'v' next to all veggie-friendly options. Genius.

Top five cheap eats

The Bread Stop – Cheap and cheerful food to fill you up.

Pizza Volante – Lunchtime offers in a dinnertime atmosphere. Classy.

Balti King – Love it or hate it, there's no denying its value.

Wokmania – All you can eat. And you will eat a lot.

Las Iguanas – Eat before 6.30pm to get the best deals.

Top five places for a posh meal

The Dam House – Damn fine food in a damn fine setting.

The Showroom Café – combine with a flick to impress a date.

Piccolinos – Service of the highest, continental order.

Nonnas – Out of town, but worth the journey.

Hui Wei – Chinese food has never seemed so chic and stylish.

How to get your meal for *Free*

'THE BEST THINGS IN LIFE ARE FREE', SANG JANET JACKSON AND LUTHER VANDROSS. AND WHO ARE WE TO ARGUE WITH SOMEONE WHO HAS THE WORD 'DROSS' IN THEIR SURNAME? HERE, THEN, ARE ITCHY'S TIPS FOR GETTING YOUR MEAL FOR FREE WHEN DINING OUT

Take offence – What do they mean they're a steak restaurant? You're a vegetarian, goddammit, and the very presence of a piece of meat on your plate constitutes a grave slur against your lifestyle. Though a free meal might stop you calling your animal rights activist mates.

Spot a 'rodent' – Bag yourself some form of wind-up animal toy, and unleash it across the floor of your restaurant. As soon as you release, leap up screaming 'Mouse! Mouse!' in the most hysterical voice you can manage. Have an accomplice waiting to retrieve the toy in the confusion, and they'll have to let you off paying to make it up to you.

Make up a stupid food allergy Food allergies are all the rage nowadays; you can get away with pretending you're allergic to pretty much anything. Make up an allergy to something suitably ludicrous, then nip to the toilets, inflate a balloon, stuff it down the neck of your top, and draw on your face with red felt tip. Hey presto: instant swollen throat and rash. They're bound to give you a freebie after doing all that to poor old you.

Fake narcolepsy – Every time the waiter attempts to present you with the bill, pretend to drop off. No way can they charge you if they can't rouse you. Sooner or later they'll give up and carry you out onto the street, where you can sneak away with a belly as full as your wallet.

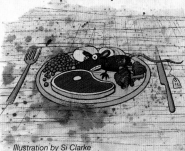

Illustration by Si Clarke

Eat

CAFÉS

Big Sandwich Shop and Cafeteria

285 Middlewood Road

(0114) 220 3899

'Not another café', we hear you cry in desperation, tormented by visions of builders' arses and dour waitresses flicking fag ash into your tea. But this one is a café with a twist. It specialises in Polish food. They know how to do a good feed, and with foods like pierogis (Polish dumplings), this is stodgy grub at its very best. They even offer a buffet, if a single serving of Hungarian goulash isn't enough to get you straight through the door.

☻ Mon–Sat, 9am–5pm

🍴 Pierogi, £3.50

Café Euro

72 John Street

(0114) 273 8553

Hippies beware: this place is going to be your brand new home from home (or from the garden you so lovingly frolic through barefooted). In fairness, Café Euro is not just for the earth-adoring, dreadlock-sporting and kaftan-wearing types among us, it's also for all of those who care about doing the right thing. They serve only organic and Fairtrade products, right down to the slices of bread your beansprouts are embedded in. So you can feel proud of the fact you're eating your way to a better globe.

☻ Mon, 9am–5pm; Tue–Fri, 10am–9pm; Sat, 10am–6pm; Sun, 10am–4pm

🍴 Eat-in veggie sandwich, £2.50

The Bread Stop

296 Ecclesall Road

(0114) 266 1500

More than once in your life, you will find yourself skipping meal after meal for of an unending list of reasons: you're late for lectures – no breakfast; your hangover has continued into the afternoon – no lunch; you've poisoned your best friend and have but minutes to find a cure – no dinner. There's just no time. Unless, that is, you nip out to The Bread Stop and pick up a delicious sandwich or pasta salad to order, with choices ranging from all-day breakfast baps to roast pork baguettes. Very satisfying. And your friend may yet live.

☻ Mon–Sat, 8.30am–5pm

🍴 Roast pork and apple sandwich, regular £2.20; large, £2.60

Café Uno

631–633 Ecclesall Road

(0114) 267 2565

From the décor it's not likely you'd make the mistake of thinking you might be sat in a bistro in Italy. But keep your eyes closed through the meal, and the smell, sounds and taste could quite possibly take you there, although the company you're dining with might think you're acting strangely. The tables are crammed in but the lively atmosphere means you still can't hear your neighbours' conversations, no matter how hard you try. It's busy, but an air of intimacy remains; amazing what a candle in the middle of the table can do eh?

☻ Mon–Sat, 10am–11pm; Sun, 11am–10pm

🍴 Pollo alla pizzalola, £10.95

🍷 £11.95

Coffee Moco

202 West Street

(0114) 276 7474

As the sandwich boom continues and we're overrun by Subways and Starbucks, take refuge in this unassuming coffee house-cum-trendy venue that actually feels quite nicely human. You can find lunch-time snacks that taste authentic rather than plastic, and combinations such as Brie and mango will have you too confused to say no. Suffice to say, vegetarians will find a haven here, but so will anyone willing to spend under a fiver on some lunch that tastes more like food and less like a conglomerate.

🕒 *Mon–Fri, 8am–8pm; Sat, 8am–6pm;*
Sun, 10am–4pm

🍴 *Brie & mango baguette, £3*

Magellan's Café

The Quadrant, 99 Parkway Avenue

(0114) 227 0005

You've never seen anything like it – It's new, it's exciting... erm, not really, no it's not. We apologise for the misleading opening line, but really we needed to grab your attention and we knew if we said, 'They serve hot and cold sandwiches on a buffet line', it just might not do the trick. So we tricked you, but give us some points for originality – at least we didn't just write 'tits!'. This place is no gourmet deal, but if you're looking for a cheap sandwich that you could've maybe made yourself, we couldn't think of anywhere better to go.

🕒 *Mon–Sun, 8am–10am & 12pm–2pm;*
snacks, 'til 4pm

🍴 *Cheese panini, £2*

Eat

Scott's Pantry

321 Glossop Road
(0114) 276 0232

There seem to be about 20 Subways in Sheffield and they're all within a 50-metre radius of one another. You can't move for meatball marinaras. Places like Scott's Pantry are fighting the battle against such stale super-companies. Scott's is located very close to the university and feeds many hungry students, workmen and the office crowd. They have an excellent selection of filling and freshly made sarnies ranging from the interesting (feta cheese) to the classic (sausage and ketchup). They also sell other snacks and cakes, all at student-friendly prices.

☺ Mon–Sat, 7.30am–3pm
🍴 Bacon and chicken mayo sarnie, £1.70

Twenty Two A

22a Norfolk Row
(0114) 276 7462

When it comes to birthdays, nothing makes your heart sink faster than the two phrases, 'good things come in small packages' and 'it's the thought that counts'. Everybody knows these are just polite ways of labelling somebody a skinflint and thinly concealing your bitter disappointment. When it comes to the Twenty Two A café, however, never a truer word was spoken. Its size and popularity may make it feel a little cramped at times, but the delicious homemade food and the thoughtful finishing touches to the décor easily justify making the trip there and squeezing inside.

☺ Mon–Thu, 8am–5pm; Fri–Sat, 8am–7pm
🍴 Potato wedges with salad and dip, £3.95

Woody's Sandwich Bar

657 Ecclesall Road
(0114) 267 6122

Bored of your usual ham sandwich? Searching for another relish to fill that void between your slices of bread? Worry no longer, as Woody's has more fillings than you can shake a bread stick at. This does, however, have the undesired effect of creating a sense of panic as you stand dumbstruck in awe at blackboard after blackboard of options. Better think quick; the whole of Ecclesall Road is forming a queue behind you and they have minus 30 minutes before the end of their lunch. No pressure though.

☺ Mon–Fri, 8.30am–4pm; Sat, 9am–4pm; Sun, 10am–3pm
🍴 £1.50–£4

RESTAURANTS

Alfie+Bella

46 Howard Street
(0114) 270 0101

You know what a pizza is, and chances are by now, you know what a good pizza is. So do we, and here at Itchy we love a good pizza. Mmmm, with meat toppings like pepperoni and sausages and Parma ham slices and... alright, so this review may have deteriorated into a bit of a reverie on flesh products, but the point is these guys make a good pizza and they have a whole array of toppings to choose from, even for the less carnivorous of us.

🄲 *Café, Mon–Fri, 8am–3pm; delivery, Thu, 6pm–9.30pm; Fri–Sat, 6pm–11pm*
🄸 *12" meatball pizza, £7.95*

Ask

8–10 Cambridge Street
(0114) 273 0073

It's inevitable that any day now Ask will be taking the crown from Pizza Express as the 'slightly upmarket Italian chain restaurant' king. And it's no surprise really. Ask offers a delicious range of both pizza and pasta and creates an atmosphere that feels perfect for any occasion. Sure, you may feel like a cheap corporate whore when there's so many independent Italians lining the streets of Sheffield, but selling your soul to the devil is a small price to pay for Ask's chicken and mushroom oven baked pasta.

🄲 *Mon–Thu, 12pm–10pm; Fri–Sat, 12pm–11.30pm; Sun, 12pm–10.30pm*
🄸 *Penne con pollo al forno, £7.95*
🄶 *£11.95*

Antibo

West 1, Unit 10, The Plaza 8, Fitzwilliam Street
(0114) 272 7222

When dining in Antibo you may feel that, like Julia Roberts in *Pretty Woman*, you should have got some training on how to use the correct cutlery. This place is posh. The grand interior and Roman artwork will have you feeling like you've won the lottery, but thankfully the prices are equivalent to a fairly lucky day at the dogs, so you don't have to be a millionaire to eat here. The atmosphere is by no means intimidating; the size of the waiter's pepper grinder, however, is.

🄲 *Mon–Thu, 12pm–2.30pm & 5pm–11pm; Fri–Sat, 12pm–2.30pm & 5pm–11.30pm*
🄸 *Tagliatelle pollo piccante, £9.75*
🄶 *£14.95*

Eat

Baan Thai

1 Ecclesall Road

(0114) 275 4800

The King of Thailand must be pretty peeved. Someone's only gone and stolen a few choice items from his palace and used them to transform this old bank into a classy Thai restaurant. Ok, so on closer inspection you may be able to see the gold on the statues beginning to peel, but you get the idea. It's grand in the nicest, tackiest way possible. Home to the biggest menus in the world and the politest waiting staff, this place will have you feeling all Leonardo DiCaprio-like, wanting to jet off to some Thai beach.

🕒 *Mon–Sun, 12pm–2.30pm & 6pm–11pm*

🍴 *Gaeng garee gai (yellow curry), £7.95*

💷 *£10.25*

Balti King

216 Fulwood Road

(0114) 266 6655

The Balti King does exactly what it says on the tin: cooks up the king of baltis. The place has established itself as a firm student and celebrity favourite, with David Blunkett, Sean Bean and Vinnie Jones having passed through its doors. With over 250 dishes and speedy, friendly service, it's easy to see why *The Independent* rated it amongst its top 50 places to visit in Sheffield. Its late night opening times make it the perfect place to visit as you stumble back from Skool Disco at Corporation.

🕒 *Mon–Thu, 12pm–3am; Fri–Sat, 12pm–4am; Sun, 12pm–2am*

🍴 *Chicken and garlic balti, £5.50*

💷 *£9.95*

BB's Italian Restaurant

119 Devonshire Street

(0114) 279 9394

'When the moon hits your eye/Like a big pizza pie/That's amore. When the world seems to shine/Like you've had too much wine/That's amore.' This song was clearly written about BB's. How do we know? Firstly, they have lovely big pizza pies. Secondly, everybody in there has probably had too much wine, and alcohol-soaked dishes such as Malibu chicken and Sambuca pancakes litter the menu to make sure those who haven't don't get away with it. And finally, everyone who visits BB's always comes back for a-more.

🕒 *Mon–Sat, 5.30pm–10.30pm*

🍴 *Pollo al Malibu, £10.30*

💷 *BYO*

Bitz & Pizza Bar and Restaurant

Valley Centertainment, Broughton Lane

(0114) 242 6676

Like many of the restaurants in Centertainment, this one falls into the category of 'bland and soulless'. The food is ok, the staff usually say their 'pleases and thank yous and the title gives you an idea of the eclectic menu. Sadly, the minimal style applies to more than just the décor. We've seen more atmosphere and enthusiasm in a juvenile detention centre (on telly, of course). Despite all its bad qualities, it's still the best place in the barren valley of Centertainment.

🕒 *Sun–Thu, 12pm–9.30pm; Fri–Sat, 12pm–10pm*

🍴 *Penne Alfredo, £8.15*

💷 *£11.45*

Champs Sports Bar and Restaurant
315–319 Ecclesall Road
(0114) 266 6333

We like this place as much as the Beckhams love a good look in a nice, long (thin) mirror. Started by sports enthusiasts, it takes its food seriously, and, for Yanks, they're not afraid to draw from their surroundings – they do English bangers and mash as well as they do greasy cheeseburgers. Prices are reasonable and the bar is separate from the restaurant, so go and line your stomach with a fat steak then get sloshed next door.

🕓 *Sun–Thu, 11.30am–11.30pm; Fri–Sat, 11.30am–12am; food, Sun–Thu, 11.30am–9.30pm; Fri–Sat, 11.30am–10pm*

🍴 *Burritos, £6.50*

💰 *£12.50*

Café Rouge
383–385 Ecclesall Road
(0114) 268 2232

This place is like that perfect pair of jeans that you keep in the back of your wardrobe. You've got so many new pairs, but these ones always seem to make a reappearance. Why? Because they do their job well. Same goes with Café Rouge, where they know how to make you feel like the sophisticated version of yourself you always suspected you could be. Good coffee and smart atmosphere have nothing on the dessert list. We are not responsible if those old jeans don't fit after one visit.

🕓 *Mon–Sat, 9am–11pm; Sun, 10am–10pm*

🍴 *Paupiette de poulet (chicken stuffed with Brie), £12*

💰 *£11.75*

East One Noodle Bar
West One Plaza, 8 Fitzwilliam Street
(0114) 272 5533

Oh dear. You've only got £6.50 left to spend on food this week. And it's Thursday. Value tuna? 10p beans? That bit of cheese which may as well be algae? No, ignore all of these; save them for next week. Today you'll eat in style, and you'll eat enough for the bloody weekend. This noodle haven hidden away under the West One flats provides mammoth portions; woolly, soupy, noodley and, most importantly, filling. Now the only problem is stretching the £3.50 alcohol budget.

🕓 *Mon–Sat, 12pm–2.30pm & 5.30pm–11pm; Sun, 1pm–11pm*

🍴 *Wonton noodle soup, £6.35*

💰 *£8.95*

Eat

Cubana

34 Trippet Lane
(0114) 276 0475

Most of us know someone who owns a Che Guevara T-shirt. Many of these will know almost nothing of Cuban revolutionaries. However, nobody can doubt Cubana's credentials. This theme restaurant serves tapas-tastic Spanish and South-American cuisine, and also hosts a variety of music nights including salsa and Latin American. It's all set in an authentically-styled restaurant with an air of faded elegance. Plonked in a drizzly back-street in Sheff.

🕒 *Mon–Thu, 5pm–12am; Fri, 5pm–1am; Sat, 12pm–1am; Sun, 12pm–12am; food, Mon–Sun, 'til 10.30pm*

🍴 *Croquetas de pescado, £4.75*

💰 *£11.95*

Felicini

509–523 Ecclesall Road
(0114) 263 1617

This is not Italian food like ol' grandmamma used to make. In fact, ol' grandmamma might well be turning in her grave at the food served here. And that's because rather than your big hearty Bolognese meals you get stylish, sophisticated nuovo Italian. Tell you what though, it tastes bellissimo. The chic interior is a good match for the food, with numerous mirrors being used to perfection and creating an overall cosmopolitan feel. It's just totally divine darling.

🕒 *Mon–Sat, 12pm–10pm, (open from 10am for coffee); Sun, 12pm–10pm*

🍴 *Chicken breast, £11.95*

💰 *£12.50*

Damon's

2 Sevenair Road
(0114) 251 1820

This place does American food right, and pride themselves on making their food fresh to order, so if you order a rack of ribs, they won't have come frozen in a plastic bag. Which is always nice. Open for breakfast, lunch, and dinner, this place is an all-day treat, and we recommend you head down for a burger immediately. Their combo platter is a special treat since you can put it together yourself. Never mind all that flailing around with Black & Decker multi-tools at the top of ladders – this is the sort of DIY we're talking about.

🕒 *Mon–Sun, 9am–11pm*

🍴 *Combo platter, £11.45*

💰 *£11.95*

Frankie and Benny's

Unit 8, Valley Centertainment, Broughton Lane
(0114) 256 1138

Mmm, warm chocolate brownie, chocolate sauce, ice cream, chocolate malt balls, toffee crunch and mountains of cream, all in one delicious dessert. The Boston Brownie at this Italian-American diner is simply divine. Or how about the Giant Cookie Sandwich? Or Mamma's Apple and Blackberry Crumble? Ok, so the Alfredo sauce on your pasta may be so overcooked it has the consistency of cold semolina, but everyone's favourite course is the dessert anyway, so who cares about the mains?

🕒 *Mon–Sat, 12pm–11pm; Sun, 12pm–10.30pm*

🍴 *Oven-baked chicken parmigana, £10.45*

💰 *£10.95*

Ha! Ha! Bar & Canteen

St Pauls Chambers, 8–12 St Pauls Parade

(0114) 276 6710

An Englishman, an Irishman and a Scotsman are going out for a meal. The Scotsman says 'Ah'd like tae eat inna cheap restaurant in the centre o' Sheffield'. The Englishman says 'I'd like the food to be a cross between home-cooked food and Jamie Oliver. I want a fish-finger sandwich in focaccia bread served with torn basil and drizzled with olive oil.' The Irishman says, 'And oi wanna have a cocktail wiv me meal and a bit of a dance afterwards'. Guess where they end up? Here! Funny, no?

☻ *Mon & Wed, 10am–11pm; Thu–Sat, 10am–12am; Sun, 10am–10.30pm*

☝ *Free range eggs and skinny chips, £5.50*

✆ *£10.95*

La Terrazza

352 Sharrowvale Road

(0114) 268 5150

A sophisticated bistro that could have been snapped up off the pavements of Italy? If that's what you're after, then don't go here. The décor is nothing special, (in fact nothing inside the restaurant really is), and yet there's always a good atmosphere. This is due in large part to the contented fullness of the diners who have just eaten a bloomin' fine meal at a bloomin' fine price, served by an 'Italian' manager who looks and sounds like he might burst into a spout of Cockney rhyming slang at any moment.

☻ *Mon–Sat, 6pm–11pm; Sun, 6.30pm–11pm*

☝ *Mafiosa pizza, £6.50*

✆ *£9.50*

Huiwei by Simply Chinese

221 Glossop Road

(0114) 201 3482

This place is authentically Chinese, but how do we know? Chopsticks, that's how. You'd better be a proficient user of them unless you want to go through the embarrassment of asking for a knife and fork. And so you'll sit trying to master the art, feeling immensely proud when you manage to get a pea in your mouth. Still, it's all bloody good fun as you watch your mates flick rice into their laps. Plus the surroundings are so stylish you won't mind that it takes you two hours to eat your meal.

☻ *Mon–Fri, 12pm–2pm & 5pm–11pm; Sat–Sun, 5pm–11pm*

☝ *Simply sweet & sour chicken, £6.95*

✆ *£11.95*

Eat

Las Iguanas

West One Plaza, 8 Fitzwilliam Street

(0114) 252 1010

So you want to be all Ricky Martin and start living the vida loca, eh? But where could satisfy those Latin cravings? Las Iguanas, that's where. As you seat yourself at a mosaic-topped table, the aromas of authentic food fill the air. While choosing from the top notch menu, you'll glance around at the Latino artefacts, wondering how the hell they managed to get most of them back through customs. And after knocking back a few cachaças, you'll be wiggling your hips like ol' Ricky himself.

🕙 *Mon–Thu, 12pm–11pm; Fri–Sat, 12pm–11.30pm; Sun, 12pm–10.30pm*

🍴 *Chicken fajitas, £11.50*

💰 *£12.50*

Mama's and Leonie's

111 Norfolk Street

(0114) 272 0490

An old style restaurant just like your favourite cousin Tony used to work in (if your cousin's Italian and a pizza chef, that is). An intimate atmosphere inside actually means you're almost sat on your neighbour's lap; but when that neighbour happens to be an Italian beauty or a passing star from the nearby Crucible theatre, you may not mind so much. Just take care not to flirt when you've got the other half of your dinner splattered around your face. Not a good look.

🕙 *Mon–Thu, 9.30am–11pm; Fri–Sat, 9.30am–11.30pm*

🍴 *Cannelloni al forno, £7.85*

💰 *£10.95*

Maranello's

438 Ecclesall Road

(0114) 266 5491

Fresh fish delivered daily, cooked to perfection like all the other meals on offer. This is Italian food so good that you wouldn't be foolish for wondering whether it had actually been air-lifted over from Florence that minute. No, the time you'll feel foolish is when your knife clangs to the floor after falling off the inappropriately small table. And when the numerous diners are disturbed and turn round to stare as you bashfully accept a new one. Still, if you're lucky the waiter will save your blushes.

🕙 *Tue–Sat, 5.30pm–11.30pm; Sun, 12pm–10.30pm*

🍴 *Marluzzo Fiorentina, £14.20*

💰 *£11.90*

Mei's Chinese

19 Charles Street

(0114) 275 6041

We don't know about you, but we like our Chinese food proper. That means none of that 'all-you-can-eat' fried rubbish, but authentic cuisine; trying (and failing) to eat with chopsticks; and real Chinese people running the show. The underground location swallows you up in all things China-like, so much so that you'll emerge into the delightful Sheffield streets expecting to see Kowloon stretching out in front of you. Alas, it's only Sheffield. Oh well, you'll get over the disappointment.

☻ *Tue–Fri, 12pm–2pm & 5.30pm–11pm; Sat–Sun, 12pm–11pm*

🍴 *Chicken chow mein, £5.50*

✪ *£10*

Nando's

Unit C Royal Plaza Development, West Street

(0114) 278 0044

'Chick, chick, chick, chick, chicken' is what you'll be getting here, so if you fancy a slab of beef it wouldn't be the wisest choice of venue. Everyone's been to a Nando's by now (and if you haven't, then where the hell have you been?), and now their peri-peri sauce has become famous – using regular ketchup while you're there is officially illegal. Who knows what goes into it, but whatever it is, it'll make you 'feel like Chicken Tonight, like Chicken Tonight'. Oh, so many chicken songs.

☻ *Sun–Thu, 12pm–11.30pm; Fri–Sat, 12pm–12am*

🍴 *Peri-peri chicken, £8.10*

✪ *£10.95*

The Mogul Room

282 Sharrowvale Road

(0114) 267 9846

Home to peckish revellers pitching up here after a pint or five at the neighbouring watering holes, The Mogul Room is always decent and dependable. It's been swanked up recently and is indeed fit for a Mogul (whatever one of them is). Gone is the strange but quaint conservatory-like décor and fake vines, and in their place is tasteful, modern, Indian style. The superb food will hit the spot every time, whether you're visiting as a drunken reveller or sophisticated diner. Moguls all round.

☻ *Sun–Thu, 5.30pm–11.30pm; Fri–Sat, 5.30pm–12.30am*

🍴 *Red sea bream, £14*

✪ *£10.95*

Nonna's

537–541 Ecclesall Road

(0114) 268 6166

If you could capture the essence of Italy in a building and make a successful business out of it, then Nonna's would be it. An Italian stallion in the restaurant world, it attracts quite a discerning crowd. You'll see them of an evening sat outside with a glass of Chardonnay, dipping their bread into olive oil, watching poor students on their way to Tesco to buy some value baked beans and trying to hit them with their stuffed olives. Ok, we made that last bit up.

☻ *Mon–Thu, 12pm–3.30pm & 6pm–9.30pm; Fri–Sat, 12pm–3.30pm & 6pm–10pm; Sun, 12pm–9pm*

🍴 *Filetto, £18.95*

✪ *£21.95*

Eat

Noodle King

639 Ecclesall Road

(0114) 266 4477

The King was in his counting house, counting out his money, his noodles sold so well you see, it really was quite funny. The chefs were in the kitchen, there for all to see, filling up the diners, who were happy as could be. The stomachs of the diners were just as happy too, the dishes were so cheap that you could eat quite a few. So everyone's a winner, this place should not be missed, whether you're very sober, or completely pissed.

🕒 *Mon–Thu, 12pm–3.30pm & 5.30pm–11pm; Fri, 12pm–3.30pm & 5.30pm–11.30pm; Sat, 12pm–11.30pm; Sun, 12pm–11pm*

🍴 *Thai green curry with chicken, £5.60*

💰 *£9.50*

Piccolino

4 Millennium Square

(0114) 275 2698

No, not the small wooden boy whose nose had a strange tendency to grow; vastly different spelling, friends. Instead it's yet another Italian restaurant to add to Sheffield's gems. This one takes on the guise of an American, open plan, airy loft apartment type place, while cunningly being on the ground floor. 'Eh?', you may well be thinking – best go check it out for yourself. Plus there's loads of room to sit and eat outside – in the words of potty-mouthed Lily Allen – we believe that is called al fresco.

🕒 *Mon–Sat, 12pm–11pm; Sun, 12pm–10.30pm*

🍴 *Trofiette al pollo, £9.50*

💰 *£13.75*

The Pasta Bar

270 Sharrow Vale Road

(0114) 268 0505

Now, this place could have been called Perfect Pasta, or Bellissimo or Mmm the Food Here is Great. What, not catchy enough? Well, the main point is that the name doesn't really reflect what goes on inside. More of an intimate café than a bar, it's certainly worth stepping in from off the pavement. The menu isn't massive but boy, what's on it is lip-lickingly good. So much so in fact that you won't care about splattering it all over your face in your haste to get it in your mouth quicker.

🕒 *Thu–Sun, 12pm–3pm; Tue–Sun, 5pm–10pm*

🍴 *Zucchini pancetta, £9*

💰 *£13*

Pizza Express

124 Devonshire Street

(0114) 275 2755

Your average establishment in the Devonshire Quarter area of Sheffield is fresh, original and effortlessly cool. A quick glance through the big glass doors at Pizza Express with its stainless steel interiors and 'just for show' grand piano, and it's obvious that this restaurant is trying far too hard to be 'in' with the 'in crowd'. Like the embarrassing uncle who likes to refer to you as 'homie' or throw words like 'emo' or 'gangsta' into the conversation to prove he's still 'down wit' da kids', (his words, not ours), Pizza Express is cringeworthy.

🕒 *Mon–Sun, 12pm–11pm*

🍴 *Il Padrino Pizza, £8.95*

💰 *£11.75*

Pizza Hut

1–3, Berekley Precinct, Ecclesall Road

(0114) 268 0697

A Pizza Hut, a Pizza Hut, Kentucky Fried Chicken and a Pizza Hut. McDonalds, McDonalds, Kentucky Fried Chicken and a Pizza Hut. Well, we thought surely you don't need a review of this place so we sang you nice a little song instead. What? Complaints? Suit yourself, a review it is then. No denying the pizza here is alright; it's just a shame that hordes of children seem to think so too. If you don't get sat next to a load of rowdy kids screaming for a balloon, it's not too bad.

🕑 *Mon–Thu, 11.30am–10pm; Fri–Sat, 11.30am–11pm; Sun, 12pm–10pm*

🍴 *Large meat feast pizza, £11.99*

💷 *£10.99*

Que-Tal?

278–280 Glossop Road

(0114) 276 2761

When potential punters peer through the window, Que-Tal's cheap plastic table clothes, dodgy colour scheme and weird, malnourished bird/turtle mascot means it often gets overlooked amidst the abundance of eateries in this area. But here at Itchy we would never be so superficial as to judge a book by its poorly-painted and run-down cover. Every dish we've tried on its menu has been delicious, the staff are great and the atmosphere is cosy. You even start to consider the décor as homely after a couple of glasses of their tasty wine.

🕑 *Mon–Sun, 5pm–12am*

🍴 *Chimichangas with chips, £9.50*

💷 *£11.95*

Pizza Volante

255 Glossop Road

(0114) 273 9056

Is it a bird? Is it a plane? Err no, it's a pizza. Pizza volante is Italian for 'flying pizza', and if there were an Olympic competition for throwing food, then you could do worse than get a discus here. It would certainly win against weak opponents such as spaghetti and lasagne, although a well-aimed garlic bread javelin would probably challenge strongly. Pizza Volante is usually busy as a result of the excellent and affordable food and special lunchtime deals. We're pretty sure the comedy name helps too.

🕑 *Mon–Fri, 10am–2.30pm & 5.30pm–11.30pm; Sat–Sun, 5.30pm–11.30pm*

🍴 *Pizza occhio di bue, £7.50*

💷 *£10.50*

San Lorenzo

344 Sharrow Vale Road

(0114) 266 9147

In the midst of a gang of Italian restaurants, this particular one doesn't stand out as the godfather. Instead it's more like the weedy cousin who gets bullied by the rest of the mob. It seems likely it's tried to cheat in the taste bud stakes by using a few tins of pre-made tomato sauce, and yet it still fails. If you want to avoid cooking that much then this place might be acceptable. Although if you're going to be that lazy, you may as well just pop along and get a meatball sub – it does for Joey.

🕑 *Mon–Thu, 6pm–11.30pm; Fri–Sat, 6pm–12am; Sun, 6pm–11pm*

🍴 *Calzone special, £7.50*

💷 *£10.95*

Eat

The Showroom and Workstation

7 Paternoster Row

(0114) 249 5479

Dilemma: you want to treat your blind date/long-term partner/attractive 'good friend' to a nice candlelit dinner followed by the chance to get cosy in the back row of the cinema but you only have enough money to do one of the two activities. Solution: The Showroom Café. For a mere £14.95, you get a top notch meal, a glass of wine and a cinema ticket. The food is so delicious and the place looks so upmarket, that your date will never know how big a cheapskate you actually are.

🕑 Wed–Sat, 5.30pm–9pm

🍴 Seared tuna loin steak, £9.50

💰 £9.95

Wokmania

137 West Street

(0114) 275 5885

One of the first things you'll notice here are the screens constantly playing episodes of *Takeshi's Castle*. As this slightly disturbing choice of Japanese game show demonstrates, the restaurant does not stick strictly to its Chinese theme. The food consists more generally of 'Eastern' dishes, and after a while you begin to feel like a Takeshi contestant yourself, racing round the hot plates as fast as possible so you can go up for the next round in record time. Your prize at the end of all this is a full tummy and a satisfied smile.

🕑 Mon–Sat, 12pm–11pm; Sun, 12pm–10pm

🍴 Sunday buffet, £8.95

💰 £8.50

TGI Fridays

Sheffield Road

(0114) 244 3386

We are proud of our roots. We like a pint in the pub on a rainy Sunday and we wear our England shirts with pride come the World Cup. However, there are some foreign influences that we can't refuse. And a big, fat burger is one of them. We're not saying Friday's makes the best burgers this side of the Atlantic, but they do make a good one, and they gain extra points by serving them to you in crazy hats and cheesy smiles. Even us hardened Itchy folk can't help but smirk.

🕑 Mon–Sat, 12pm–11.30pm;

Sun, 12pm–11pm

🍴 Ultimate San Fran burger, £10.25

💰 £11.95

Yankees

418 Ecclesall Road

(0114) 268 0828

A big juicy burger with cheese oozing out of the sides, a dish of fries to accompany it and enough tomato ketchup to make it look like there's been a massacre on your plate. This place may make every celebrity chef turn their nose up in horror, but who cares what they think; they've sold their passion for cooking for the fickle price of fame, so shame on them. Yankees may not win food awards, but it will make you thankful for American-sized portions of food, if not your belly, after eating them.

🕑 Mon, 5pm–11.45pm;

Tue–Sun, 11.45am–11.30pm

🍴 Cheese burger, £5.60

💰 £8.99

Drink

Drink

Welcome to Drink

We all know that most happy hours last longer than an hour, a reason to be even happier. One home to happiness is **The Common Room (127–129 Devonshire Street, 0114 280 8221)**. From Monday to Friday between 5pm and 8pm you can get half price cocktails or two glasses of wine for just £3. How on earth will you decide which to have? **The Ha! Ha! Bar (8–12 St Paul's Parade, 0114 276 6710)** will have you laughing your socks off with their happy hour from 5pm–7pm giving you any cocktail for £3. At that price you can work your way through the menu, although you probably won't remember it the next day. If cocktails aren't your tipple, however, **The Harley (334 Glossop Road, 0114 275 2288)** might suit you better. Selected lagers at £2–£2.30, single and a mixer at £1.80 and a glass of wine at £2.60 between 4pm and 7pm daily will get you warmed up nicely.

Top five cocktails

Pink Russian (Bia Hoi) – A cute, fluffy twist on a classic.

Delboy (Revolution) – Far more exotic than the cockney trader.

A Bloody Strong and Northern Bloody Mary (The Old House) – Pretend you're a local and ask for this Henderson's relish drink.

Coco Cubana (Cubana) – Like a liquid toffee, South American style.

Kitten Cuddler (Champs Sports Bar) – This kitten's got claws. Let it scratch you.

Top five most notable toilets

Champs Sports Bar – Merchandise everywhere. And we mean everywhere.

Bar One – The graffiti debates range from fit bar staff to 'mooncups' (don't ask).

Bia Hoi – A giant Buddha to welcome you in.

Varsity – Very bad. There's always somebody lying on the floor in a pile of his or her own sick.

Takapuna – Never again will you feel this glamorous on the lav.

How to make your pint last all day

befriend the nearest person who looks like they might have full pockets. Drunk that one too? Tell someone you're about to become a parent. Necked that one as well? Well, there's no helping you then...

Play coin football – Fact: if you're not actually drinking, your drink lasts longer. Indulge in a nice game of coin footie instead. Place three coins in a triangle formation, then flick them forwards one by one, using the coin that's furthest back, sliding it between the other two. The target is the makeshift goal your opponent has made with his fingers

HARD UP, BUT LIKE NOTHING MORE THAN WHILING AWAY TIME IN A BOOZER? FEAR NOT. A TRIP TO THE PUB NEEDN'T BREAK THE BANK

Keep the pint cool – Get yourself one of those chemical ice-packs for injuries. After an hour or so, crack it open, and wrap it around your beverage. Hey presto: it's like you've just bought it.

Go minesweeping – Some people just don't understand the value of the last two sips. Wait 'til these wasteful types have left the pub, then nip over and finish their backwash. Take the glass to the bar afterwards, and the bar staff'll love you so much they'll let you carry on all day.

Create fake identities – Running perilously low on that pint? Quick, pretend it's your birthday and

Get a job there – Hey, we've given you four top tips already. What more do you want from us? If you can't make a pint last all day with these gems, you're going to have to ask the landlord for a job.

Illustration by Si Clarke

Drink

BARS

Bar One

University of Sheffield Students' Union, Western Bank
(0114) 222 8500

Sheffield University's Bar One apparently has the longest student bar in the country. This means it doesn't take long to get a cheap pint from the moody staff. There's a large pool room and big-screen TVs for sports fixtures and *Neighbours*. Eat a Wimpy-esque takeaway in the dubious One To Go or chill in the beer garden. Best avoid until the evening when it fills up with students, many dressed as pirates/cheerleaders/retro television characters for one of the many union nights.

☺ *Mon–Thu, 11am–12am; Fri–Sat, 11am–1am; Sun, 12pm–12am; food, all day*

Bar S1

240 West Street
(0114) 279 8018

Big Bird, Batman and Bo Peep have all been spotted downing a few cocktails here. This is not because the cheap alcohol induces vivid hallucinations of childhood heroes, but more likely because the cheap alcohol makes this a favourite stop for fancy dress bar crawls. You'll often see Snow White and a few dwarfs huddled round what used to be a fire place, squashed into the booth-style seating next to a Roman soldier and Captain Jack Sparrow. It's like a cheap alternative to Disneyland without the rides or the child-friendly censorship.

☺ *Sun–Wed, 12pm–12am; Thu–Sat, 12pm–1am; food, Mon–Sun, 12pm–8pm*

🍴 *Lamb shank with mashed potato, £6.25*

Bai Hoi

1 Mappin Street
(0114) 279 9250

Buddha didn't view drinking vast quantities of trendy vodka as the true way to gain enlightenment. So quite why there is a giant Buddha watching over drunken punters in Bia-Hoi is a bit of a mystery. Take a quick break from your bar-crawl down West Street to check out the eastern themed Buddha bar and ponder the meaning of life while queuing to buy a drink. Buddha advised the path of compassion and generosity in order to lead a happier life... so that'd be your round then.

☺ *Thu–Sat, 11am–1am; Sun–Wed, 11am–12.30am; food, Mon–Sun, 12pm–8pm*

🍴 *Big fat Buddha burger, £5.95*

💰 *£10*

The Cavendish

220–238 West Street

(0114) 252 5781

The king of the mediocre bar scene; if this place was a band, it'd be Snow Patrol. As part of the Scream chain, it offers relatively cheap drinks in a nice setting, with the usual things you'd expect to find in your local bar; a couple of pool tables, a fruit machine and plenty of big leather sofas. There's nothing particularly bad about the Cavendish (except the queues at the bar on a Saturday night, but again, that's to be expected when they sell booze at these prices), there's just nothing particularly special about it either. Unless you're reading this very review and they simultaneously play a Snow Patrol song...

Ⓒ *Mon–Sun, 12pm–12am*

The Common Room

127–129 Devonshire Street

(0114) 280 8221

'Dear Deirdre, please help me. I have not slept with a family member or anything like that, but I am currently suffering an unfulfilled social life due to my over-demanding nature. I'd like a bar that has a happy hour, 12 full-sized pool tables, screens showing all major sporting events, decent grub and internet connection, all placed in a trendy environment that's open past 11pm. I know this is a lot to ask. What can I do?' Deirdre: Get to The Common Room, you imbecile, and stop wasting my time.

Ⓒ *Mon–Sun, 11am–12.30am; food, Mon–Sun, 12pm–9pm*

Ⓜ *The Mexican beef burger, £6*

Ⓟ *£8.95*

Drink

Dam House Bar and Restaurant

Mushroom Lane

(0114) 267 6551

The Dam House overlooks Crookes Valley park and lake and has a splendid beer garden. On a hot summer day you can sit on the terrace and watch the occasional boating team take to the water. While sipping on your glass of Pimms, one could take an utterly wild leap of imagination and pretend one was having a simply spiffing time at the Royal Henley Regatta, rah rah rah. Well I say. The Dam House serves a jolly good selection of English, Italian and French food, though it's none too cheap.

ⓒ *Sat, 11am–12pm; Sun–Fri, 11am–11pm*

ⓘ *Pan fried lamb, £13*

ⓩ *£13*

DQ

Fitzwilliam Street

(0114) 221 1668

DQ is all about the music. This is a good thing because it doesn't have the welcoming atmosphere of your average friendly local. The décor is a cross between a health spa and an asylum, with cold white walls and minimal amounts of furniture. Thankfully, despite appearances, this place isn't full of women getting facials, or lunatics. The late bar hosts varied and eclectic music nights which cater especially for people who want a night out where they don't have to listen to Fedde Le Grande or Timbaland. Expect a few trilbies, hoodies and a flat-cap thrown in here and there.

ⓒ *Fri–Sat, 9pm–4am; Mon, Wed–Thu & Sun, 10pm–3am*

The Dog and Partridge

56 Trippet Lane

(0114) 249 0888

If you think it's hard to find a decent Irish bar in Sheffield – apart from on St Patrick's Day when everyone seems to jump on the bandwagon – then pay this place a visit. It's a lil' ol' Irish gem that's rumoured to sell the best Guinness in town. Established many moons ago, the place doesn't appear to have been touched since it opened. But rather than having a moth-eaten look, this just embellishes its charm. Plus if you like a spot of live music, grab your fiddle and get jamming with the regulars. They probably won't thank you for it, though. And neither will the customers.

ⓒ *Mon–Sat, 11.30am–11pm;*
Sun, 12pm–10.30pm

The Forum Cafe Bar

127–129 Devonshire Street

(0114) 272 0569

Often considered one of the better places to get your groove on, The Forum plays hosts to some great nights where the people who know that they've got the moves rock up to show them off with precision to the solid beats of the DJs. We like this place, so we guess we can cope with a bit of poetry along the way too. You might feel like you've taken a small step (or a giant leap in some cases) up in the trendiness stakes from the moment you walk through the door, and that's ok, because for one magical night, we can all be just as cool as The Forum lets us believe we are.

ⓒ *Mon–Thu, 10am–1am; Fri–Sat, 10am–2am; Sun, 11am–1am*

The Green Room

150–154 Devonshire Street

(0114) 249 3329

In terms of the area and its surrounding competitors, The Green Room seems to offer little in the way of practical enjoyment. Paying well over the odds for your drinks never seems particularly conducive to a decent evening out, and even a very good selection of bottled beer or fine wine won't make up for it (neither can it challenge neighbours The Cat or Bungalow & Bears). But no one goes to The Green Room for the price of drinks, or even the somewhat unaccommodating bar staff. They go to look cool and sound like they're backstage on *Friday Night with Jonathan Ross*. Don't they?

🕒 *Mon–Sun, 12pm–12am*

Platillos

Unit 4, Leopold Square

(0114) 276 3141

Dave and Alan decided to go to Platillos one night; they were feeling particularly trendy, you see. A few hours and numerous pints later, Dave turned to Alan suddenly and said, 'Blimey, think I've had enough to drink mate, I can see plates before my eyes'. Alan turned to where Dave was looking and said 'Me too, I can see loads of them', So, off they went home to recover from their alcoholic hallucinations. If only they had known there was really a wall full of plates as part of the quirky décor, they could have stayed for another couple of pints without fear of plate eye. Shame.

🕒 *Sun–Thu, 11am–12am;*
Fri–Sat,11am–2am

The Old House

113–117 Devonshire Street

(0114) 276 0569

Fancy a cocktail? Or two? Or 12? Either way, The Old House knows how to make a sublime tipple. Specialising in simple yet classy alcohol-based indulgences, the guys here know what they're doing. But you don't have to feel out of place if martinis aren't you're thing. The Old House's motto is 'mi casa es su casa' and you will feel at home here, regardless of what drinks you have in your hand. And a bit of a boogie will be on the cards because they like to play music that'll get you out of your seat

🕒 *Mon–Sat, 12pm–1am;*
Sun, 12pm–12.30am

🍴 *Chunky chips with dips, £3*

💷 *£13*

Drink

Lava Lounge

140–144 West Street

(0114) 276 3271

Like the final episode of *Deadwood*, Lava Lounge is a bit of an anticlimax. The name conjures up images of a dark and sensuous den, full of smouldering guests loafing around on large and luxurious sofas. This should be a place where exotic and mysterious femme fatales sip cocktails from frosted glasses before being seduced by tall, dark and handsome men with fashionable stubble. The exterior of Lava Lounge hints at this alluring fantasy as you stroll curiously down West Street. However, reality swiftly intrudes as you realise upon entry that it's actually a fairly generic wine bar.

Ⓒ *Mon–Sat, 12pm–1.30am*

The Museum

25 Orchard Street

(0114) 275 5016

Hidden behind the sprawling cobbles of Fargate, you'll find the calmer, quainter pastures of Orchard Square, possibly Sheffield's greatest spot for people-watching (or, if you rather, stalking). Whatever your motives, settle down and take your seat outside The Museum on a sunny day and observe with glee the Sheffield natives going about their lives. Aside from some pretty good beer, The Museum acts as a pit stop from the Grand Prix of stress that is the middle of town. Note the potential for fooling others into thinking you're actually getting cultured.

Ⓒ *Mon–Thu, 11am–11pm; Fri–Sat, 11am–12am; Sun, 12pm–10.30pm*

The Porter Cottage

286 Sharrowvale Road

(0114) 268 7412

What's that hideous music playing? You've walked into the Porter Cottage and some idiot has put on something god-awful. Just because there's a brilliantly varied selection on one of the best jukeboxes in Sheffield, doesn't mean every song on it has to be played. Console yourself with one of the fresh, well-kept ales on offer, and take comfort in the fact that it will take no time at all to get served by the numerous, well-mannered bar staff. Don't worry, the Sugababes will end soon. Then you can rock out to Depeche Mode or Erasure. Or something.

Ⓒ *Mon–Thu, 5.30pm–11.30pm; Fri, 5.30pm–12am; Sat, 7pm–12am; Sun 7pm–11pm*

The Red Lion

109 Charles Street

(0114) 272 4997

Ignore your first impressions of The Red Lion and make an effort to step inside. From the outside, it may look like a localised old-codger hive, filled with people that have been drinking since 1968 and haven't yet left. In reality, it's home to a set of the most accommodating bar people this side of Rotherham, with well-kept beer to boot. A place to take old friends to, the very brave will stray into the often empty but quaint lounge bar and be rewarded with a perfect quiet-pint haven. Just be careful you're not still there in 40 years' time.

🍷 *Mon–Fri, 12pm–11pm; Sat, 12pm–3pm & 7pm–11pm; Sun, 12pm–3pm & 7pm-10.30pm*

RSVP

2–6 Cambridge Street

(0114) 275 5152

So what is it exactly you want from a bar? Tabletops so wet from spilled drinks they make your wallet/phone/bag/hands or anything else placed on them sticky? Perhaps you want somewhere with entertainment, like betting with your mates on which group of lads are going to start a fight first? If that's your ideal, then look no further than RSVP. Its city centre location means you might find yourself stumbling in one night, but just make sure you're wearing your beer goggles.

🍷 *Sun–Thu, 10am–12am; Fri–Sat, 10am–1am*

🍴 *Steak and ale pie, £6.75*

🥂 *£8.95*

Revolution

The Plaza, 8 Fitzwilliam Street

(0114) 273 9469

In this faux-Russian bar you can pick yourself up a Russian Bride (a White Russian cocktail with a bit of a twist) or even a pitcher of RazzPutin (a rather bitter and sour mixture). With its vast range of flavoured vodkas, you'll feel just like a kid in a candy shop. Or, to be more specific, Charlie in Willy Wonka's factory, as it's not unheard of for Oompa Loompas to be wandering round here serving you minted chocolate shots while singing their little hearts out. Seriously.

🍷 *Mon–Sat, 11.30am–12am; Sun, 12pm–12am; food, Mon–Sun, 12pm–8pm*

🍴 *Thai fishcakes, £6.95*

🥂 *Flavoured vodka shots, £1.95*

Ruskin's Wine Bar

101 Norfolk Street

(0114) 273 8255

A bit of a Pick 'n' Mix bar, Ruskin's prides itself on attracting crowds of all types and varieties. Don't be surprised to bump into your little sister's emo friend with dyed purple hair and your trendy but silly aunt Betty all on the same day. Music is the theme here. They try hard to balance conflicting tastes in a laudable attempt to bust out everyone's favourite at some point during the night, from jazz to Hed Kandi bangin' toons. The thing we wonder is whether they might get it right if they didn't try that little bit too hard.

🍷 *Mon–Thu, 11am–11.30pm; Fri–Sat, 11am–12am; Sun, 12pm–10pm*

🥂 *£12*

Drink

The South Sea
3 Spooner Road
(0114) 268 2992

This friendly little bar has recently been refurbished, and this raises it above many of the other student hovels which you'll find around Broomhill. Ok, so it's still a Scream bar, and the place looks pretty soulless from the outside, but all this is in some way redeemed by the eclectic jukebox (which has over 10,000 songs), the weekly live DJ sets and the decent discounts on food and drink. This place caters for both those looking to get rat-arsed on the cheap, and also those looking for a nice, quiet drink and some pretty decent background music.

Ⓒ Mon–Sat, 12pm–11pm;
Sun, 12pm–10.30pm

Takapuna
52–54 West Street
(0114) 272 9661

If Takapuna were a human stereotype, it'd be a modern metrosexual male. He likes to look stylish and to wear designer labels, but he keeps an eye on his finances and doesn't like to spend too much. His musical taste is eclectic and changes with the trends; he likes a bit of hip-hop, disco, house and indie. Drink-wise, he likes his beer served with a slice of lemon, cocktails with funky names or pomegranate wine spritzers. Also, he may look strangely vacant but there's probably a lot more going on upstairs than you first realise.

Ⓒ Tue & Thu–Sat, 12pm–2.30am;
Mon & Wed, 12pm–12.30am; food,
Mon–Sat, 12pm–9pm

The Swim Inn
217 Glossop Road
(0114) 252 7640

Taking its place among the other chain pubs and student boozers that line the way into West Street is this typical Wetherspoons bar. Quite why it's called The Swim Inn, we have never managed to work out, but unless all you're looking for is dead cheap beer or two for £5.99 offers on food, then you can just swim right back out again. Not that there's much wrong with The Swim Inn, it's just that we've told you about so many other places unique to the fair city of Sheff, that we reckon you could do better than to waste your time in an identi-kit bar that could have come from anywhere.

Ⓒ Mon–Sat, 9am–11pm;
Sun, 9am–10.30pm

The York
243–247 Fulwood Road
(0114) 268 8061

The one thing that makes Scream pubs so distinctive (apart from the over-use of yellow paint) is the legendary Yellow Card. Exchange a shiny pound coin for one of these and then you'll get cheap drink deals all year round. You also have the chance to win slightly pointless but nonetheless exciting prizes by collecting stamps with every drink you buy. If you collect a certain number of these stamps you might get something random, like a poster of a beaver. Of course, 'prizes' like these will only appeal to students, much like The York itself.

Ⓒ Mon–Sun, 11am–12am; food, Mon–Sun, 11am–8pm

PUBS

The Ball Inn

171–173 Crookes
(0114) 266 1211

The Ball looks down on other pubs like the king of the steel jungle. Of the many drinking holes that line the streets up here, The Ball is the best at luring in unsuspecting students and eating up their loans and overdrafts. Some people say it has a modern feel, others comment on how they like its traditional values. Some go there for the ale, others for the quiz nights, and others still for the music played at just the right volume. Somehow, The Ball is everything to everyone.

Ⓒ *Mon–Thu, 11am–11pm; Fri–Sat,*
11am–11.30pm; Sun, 12pm–10.30pm
Ⓒ *£6.50*

The Bath Hotel

66 Victoria Street
(0114) 249 5151

If ever you're on West Street, at least once please refrain from entering one of the various cheap chain pubs. After all, they have about as much soul as a morgue, and only slightly better-looking people. Instead, dive down the side street that leads you to The Bath Hotel. Aside from being able to pun your heart out telling friends where you are, you'll be able to drink premium beer in an atmosphere so local you'll forget you're in the middle of town. If you want heart, comfort and a bloody good drink, then for Christ's sake go get yourself in The Bath.

Ⓒ *Mon–Sat, 12pm–11.30pm;*
Sun, 7pm–10.30pm

Drink

Bungalows and Bears

The Old Fire Station, Division Street

(0114) 279 2901

If you go down to the bungalow today you're sure of a big surprise – that's because it's turned into a pub. Not just any pub though, but one where a tired bear can drink raspberry beer on leather sofas while playing KerPlunk and joining in the monthly knitting circle. And if music's what a bear's into, they've got more DJs and bands than you can shake a salmon at. That's if bears actually do prefer bungalows to the woods.

◉ *Sun–Thu, 12pm–12am;*
Fri–Sat, 12pm–1am

⑪ *Spinach and Yorkshire feta pie, mash and peas, £5.90*

❷ *£10.50*

Devonshire Cat

49 Wellington Street

(0114) 279 6700

'Well! I've drunk beer without a pub', thought Alice; 'but a pub without beer! That would be the most curious thing I ever saw in all my life'. The Devonshire Cat doesn't have this problem. It's a welcoming pub stocking an excellent array of beers for those with acquired tastes, with flavours such as strawberry and banana. We don't know if there's any relation between the Devonshire Cat and the Cheshire Cat, but huge grins are frequently reported on the faces of punters coming out of here.

🕐 *Mon–Thu, 11.30am–11pm; Fri–Sat, 11.30am–12am; Sun, 11.30am–10.30pm; food, Sun–Thu, 11.30am–9pm; Fri–Sat, 11.30am–8pm*

The Fox and Duck

227 Fulwood Road

(0114) 266 3422

The university-owned Fox and Duck is perfectly situated in the student-saturated area of Broomhill. And yet the pub has none of the distinguishing features of your typical student bar: sticky floors, people in fancy dress and cheesy music. Oh no. None of that here. While the students flock to neighbouring watering holes like hypochondriacs to a hospital, you'll find this place teeming with local Yorkshiremen, enjoying a few pints of bitter and discussing the finer points of pigeon racing. But with a wide selection of cask ales, it might be worth popping in to give your taste buds a bit of a treat.

🕐 *Mon–Sun, 12pm–11pm*

The Dore Moor Inn

Hathersage Road

(0114) 235 5121

Picture a traditional country pub and you'll think of open fires, big oak furniture, pictures of sheep and cows on hills and enough brassware to keep a tin of Brasso hard at it for several days. Walk in here and – ta-da! – that's exactly what you've got. Surround it with some beautiful Peak District scenery and you've got yourself a perfect stop-off point on your country drive, especially as the food arrives with lightning speed. Plenty of time left to get back out among those hills.

🕐 *Mon–Sat, 11am–11pm; Sun, 11am–10.30pm*

🍴 *8oz rump steak, £8.95*

🍷 *£10.50*

Frog and Parrot

94 Division Street

(0114) 2721280

Attend any of the band nights here and you're bound to encounter a mixture of gruff regulars perched on stools, fashion-types bobbing their bleach-blonde heads in time to the music, and students with scuffed-up Converse waving to their 'mate' in the band. The clientele is eclectic, but with its real ales and a breakfast menu which has an option of 'a bacon sarnie and a pack of Marlboros' this pub is so typically Yorkshire it hurts. The Arctic Monkeys even put a picture of it in their album cover inlay.

🕐 *Thu–Sat, 12pm–1am; Sun–Tue, 12pm–10pm; Wed, 12pm–12am; food, Mon–Sun 12pm–7pm*

🍴 *Home-made steak and ale pie, £2.99*

Drink

The Graduate
Surrey Street
(0114) 275 3767

Dirty, dirty chain pub; but being where it is, it's difficult to resist a swift drink in The Graduate. Ok, so calling it dirty is perhaps a tad harsh, but it's hard to like a place where the main gimmick is food served in what look like dog bowls. That said, the drink is cheap with the discount card, and a weekly quiz and pool tables do give it a somewhat insincere attraction. The jukebox, which is good, almost makes up for all of the above, but not quite. Sadly, even one of the best selections of tunes doesn't pull The Graduate up to the mark. Suffice to say, when you are a graduate there'll be little point in going there.

◎ *Mon–Sun, 11am–12am*

The Harley
334 Glossop Road
(0114) 275 2288

On a bar crawl around Sheffield, you're bound to encounter many bars employing a wide variety of flashy gimmicks, trying to entice you into spending all of your hard-earned money in their establishment. The Harley has no need for any of this; its entertainment and atmosphere speak for themselves. This modest bar is the place to go if you like excellent live bands, a proper good fry-up, late-night opening times, free wifi, decent DJs, any genre of music, Fairtrade coffee, reasonably-priced alcohol and friendly staff. So that's just about everybody.

◎ *Mon–Thu, 7.30am–1am; Fri, 7.30am–3am; Sat, 9am–3am; Sun, 9am–1am*

The Hadfield
26–28 Barber Road
(0114) 267 1930

The small village of Hadfield in nearby Derbyshire is better known as Royston Vasey in the sinister comedy, *The League of Gentlemen*. Luckily The Hadfield isn't a scary 'local pub for local people' filled with suspicious residents with pig noses. Instead, it's a friendly and student-orientated pub in the busy student area of Crookesmoor. It's great for live sport, with several large screens, and it also has a few pool tables. Still not convinced? Try attending one of the weekly quiz nights and you're bound to become a regular in no time.

◎ *Mon–Thu, 11.30am–11pm; Fri–Sat, 11.30am–12am; Sun, 12pm–11pm; food, Mon–Sun, 12pm–8pm*

The Howard
57 Howard Street
(0114) 278 0183

Outside, it looks like a semi-respectable, 'close to the train station' pub. Inside, it's a hive of activity, with something for everyone. Obviously, being so close to the station means that, on match days, the place overflows with middle-aged men wearing XXL football shirts and getting a little bit lairy. But if that doesn't appeal to you, keep an eye on the listings to see what up and coming bands are playing there. If you prefer your music to resonate from a turntable rather than a guitar, The Howard's Sunday trance nights are legendary.

◎ *Mon–Thu, 11am–11pm; Fri–Sat, 11am–12am; Sun, 12pm–11pm; food, Mon–Sun, 12pm–3pm & 4.30pm–7pm*

The Nursery Tavern

276 Ecclesall Road

(0114) 268 8031

The Nursery Tavern is a bit like the nurseries you may have gone to when you were three. The days when you'd play 'doctors and nurses', do a crap drawing that your parents would later pretend to like, have a nice glass of milk and then have a nap for a few hours. But instead of doctors and nurses, it's a game of 'feeling up the slapper in the boobtube', instead of milk it's a quadruple JD and Coke, and rather than a nap it's more like a comatose sprawl which needs your mates to carry you home. These slight differences aside, it's almost identical to your childhood.

🕒 *Sun–Thu, 12pm–12am;*
Fri–Sat, 12pm–1am

The Place

Nile Street

(0114) 267 1157

From the exterior this pub looks like a new build house: characterless and forgettable. But like a fine wine, over the years it has matured and become quite tasteful. Well, as tasteful as a student occupied bar can be. Offering three pool tables, a dart board and numerous big screens showing sporting events, so jocks can their get your sporting fix. Providing a decent mix of entertainment, The Place serves as a decent pre-club warm-up, and is a mere stone's throw away from the city centre. As long as you can stagger that far, you'll be fine.

🕒 *Mon–Sat, 11am–11.30pm;*
Sun, 12pm–10.30pm

Old Heavygate Inn

114 Matlock Road

(0114) 234 0003

Hidden in that little time-crevice between Crookes and Wakley, this little pub feels like it's stuck in a 1949 episode of *Corrie*. All the locals (and every single person in there is a local, and has been for the past 50 years) flock there en masse for the quiz nights, when the landlady puts on a lovely spread, including the best bread and dripping Itchy has ever tasted in a pub (although to be honest there isn't much competition). If you want to experience Yorkshire, and you've already been to the Jorvik Centre and visited the set of *Heartbeat*, then you need go no further than the Old Heavygate Inn.

🕒 *Mon–Sat, 11am–11pm; Sun, 11am–10.30pm*

Drink

The Prince of Wales

95 Ecclesall Road

(0114) 236 9176

The Prince of Wales (or Charlie to us) walks into the pub of his namesake and exclaims, 'I say, it's bloody brilliant in here. Not quite as grand as dear old home but the open fires do make it cosy. And look at the marvellously cheap menu.' (Penny-pinching is clearly how they hold on to all that taxpayers' money these days). It's a typical pub with a typical pub name, but there's a few homely extras that'll make you more than happy to while away a few nights here.

🕲 Sun–Wed, 12pm–11pm;
Thu–Sat, 12pm–12am
🍴 Steak and ale pie, £6.45
💰 £6.99

The Red Deer

18 Pitt Street

(0114) 272 2890

Ok, so when you come to step outside the view might not be the picturesque little village scene you imagined you might find yourself in as you supped warming pints of tasty ale inside the pub, but is that really such a terrible problem? Its convenient situation means you can have a sly one (alright, a few sly ones) on your lunch break and head straight back to the office. A quick breath mint and blast of deo and your boss need be none the wiser. Not that Itchy encourages drinking during working hours, of course.

🕲 Mon–Sat, 11.30am–11pm;
Sun, 7.30pm–10.30pm
🍴 Homemade quiche, £4.75

The Royal Standard

156 St Mary's Road

(0114) 272 2883

Following his (probably less than) stellar recent tour, Rod Stewart reportedly went into hiding. Worry not though lovers of the two-tone rooster-mullet-thing, we've found him posing as owner and question master of this here local. More 'standard' than 'Royal', its saving grace is that it's cheap and you can win beer tokens. But with no Penny Lancaster or Rachel Hunter in sight, 'do ya think I'm sexy?' is not a question that will be answered with a yes any time soon.

🕲 Sun–Thu, 12pm–12.30am; Fri–Sat,
11am–11pm; food, Mon–Fri, 12pm–2pm &
6pm–8pm; Sun, 2pm–6pm
🍴 Giant Yorkshire pudding, £4.95
💰 £6.75

The Springvale

1 Commonside, Steel Bank

(0114) 266 1466

Who knows who you might bump into if you visit the Springvale? Apparently, rock star Joe Cocker lived opposite and popped in now and again. Legend also has it that the Yorkshire Ripper had a drink at this pub on the night he was arrested. Reliable sources inform us that Tom Cruise met Katie Holmes over a game of pool at The Springvale. Ok, so maybe that last one was a total lie, but it was worth a try. Nowadays you're more likely to find students mixing with Crookesmoor residents, watching live sports or enjoying ale in the large beer garden.
☺ *Mon-Thu & Sun, 12pm-12.30am; Fri-Sat, 12pm-1.30am*

The White Hart

184 St Phillip Road

(0114) 272 3747

If you fancy a pub which shows off the eccentricities of local Sheffielders (and we include ourselves in that description), then The White Hart wouldn't be a bad place to start. Firstly, there are the 'amusing' mascots which line the shelves behind the bar. Secondly, there's the caricatures of locals which hang from the walls. And thirdly, there's the fact that the customers acknowledge each other in turn as they arrive at the bar, whether they've met before or not. However peculiar this lot might be though, they can put on a bloody good karaoke night.
☺ *Sun-Fri, 12pm-11pm; Sat, 11am-11pm*

Star & Garter

82 Winter Street

(0114) 272 0694

The Star & Garter is opposite Sheffield University Library and right on the boundary separating students and a local estate. It could be a potentially combustible mix, but luckily the town-gown relations in Sheffield are quite good, so students can happily discuss Chaucer alongside tattooed locals. The Star & Garter has recently changed ownership and undergone a Harvesters-style makeover. It's brighter now, but devoid of character. That said, who needs character when the pub boasts a successful weekly poker league as well as a pool table and juke-box?
☺ *Mon-Sat, 11am-1am; Sun, 11am-12am*
❼ £7.95

The West End

412 Glossop Road

(0114) 272 5871

The similarities of this pub to the West End of London are tenuous. The West End pub is next door to the Sheffield University Theatre. The West End of London has lots of theatres. The Pet Shop Boys made a song called West End Girls. The West End pub has a jukebox with two million tracks. One of which has to be the Pet Shop Boys' synth-pop classic. The West End serves cheap food and is conveniently close to the University or the Hospital. We're not sure if there are any comparisons to be made here, we just thought you should know.
☺ *Mon-Thu, 11am-11pm; Fri-Sat, 11am-12am; Sun, 12pm-11pm; food; Sun-Fri, 12pm-2.30pm*

itchy

We need hawk-eyed photographers to contribute their sparkling talents to the Itchy city guides and websites.

We want dynamic pictures of bars, pubs, clubs and restaurants in your city, as well as photos to represent the comedy, art, music, theatre, cinema and sport scenes.

If you're interested in getting involved, please send examples of your photography to: editor@itchymedia.co.uk, clearly stating which city you can work in. All work will be fully credited.

Calling all aspiring photographers

Dance

Right on Queue

DO YOU EVER FIND YOURSELF STANDING IN A LONG LINE TO ENTER A CLUB, GET A DRINK, OR GO FOR A PEE? THEN YOU'LL FIND ITCHY'S Q-TIPS ON WAYS TO AMUSE YOURSELF WHILE YOU HANG ABOUT WORTH THEIR WAIT IN GOLD

Get the party started before you even hit the floor. Just bring a bag of thick elastic bands to hand out to fellow queue-tey pies, and get everyone to pluck a different note. When you're at the bar, try blowing over the tops of bottles to entertain the other punters. If you're good enough, they might throw you enough loose change to pay for your drink.

Before striding out, get down to the pound shop and buy a big bottle of the foulest perfume you can find, or even better, nip to a fishing shop and get your mitts on a bottle of lobster essence used for scenting baits. When waiting for a loo cubicle, pretend to be a toilet attendant, and offer exiting punters a free spritz of 'fragrance'. Every pongy person you zap with your minging musk is one fewer rival to compete against in the pulling stakes.

Or you can try the following trick. Start your evening at home by chowing down on beans and bhuna. Later, when you find yourself so far back in line that the folk at the front are in a different postcode, let the gas go. Watch the crowds shrink as they run from your stink, and try to figure out who it was who let rip. Don't strain too hard though, unless you fancy wandering home with the contents of your bowels sloshing around your smalls.

Illustration by Si Clarke

CLUBS

The Casbah

1 Wellington Street

(0114) 275 6077

The Casbah has a reputation for being the place to see local bands before they make it big. We'd say this owes a lot to the Arctic Monkeys, and probably the more justified reputation is the one The Casbah has for the best club atmosphere in Sheffield. Ok, so it doesn't have as many strobe lights and fancy themed floors as Embrace, and stories of myriad scrapes and scuffles in the rough streets surrounding the club are rife, but, inside, mods, rockers, skin-headed ska lovers and long-haired hippies all get along at The Casbah's big love in.

🅒 *Times and prices vary*

Crash Club @ Hallam Union

The HUBS, Paternoster Row

(0114) 225 4111

What, not another club night catering for the 'skinny jeans and sideways hair' set? Yes indeed, this is Hallam University's contribution to the veritable whitewash of indie and rock nights that Sheffield has to offer. It may be called the Crash Club, but with the chance to check out the local talent (of the musical kind – though there are some lookers out there too) in the bar before you hit the dance floor, and an atmosphere that's a lot more fun and a lot less pretentious than some of the similar nights around the city, don't write this little baby off just yet.

🅒 *Tue, 10.30pm–2.30am*

🅐 *£3*

Corporation

Milton Street

(0114) 276 0262

At weekends, Corporation is the grungy dwelling of metal-heads and rock fans, while on Skool Disco Wednesdays, the 50p vodka and mixer offers and the poppy soundtrack means the club attracts a crowd who like their music cheesy and their outfits slutty. Rumour has it that the powers that be tried to stop their sobriety-smashing cheap alcohol deals in order to prevent a whole generation of Sheffield youngsters ending up in rehab, but Corp said no, no, no.

🅒 *Mon, 9.30pm–2.30am; Wed, 10pm–2am; Fri, 9.30pm–2.30am; Sat, 9.30pm–3am*

🅐 *Mon, £3 after 10pm; Wed, £4 or free with school uniform; Fri–Sat, £5 after 10pm*

DQ

Fitzwilliam Street

(0114) 221 1668

Your head feels like there is a small, angry creature inside, trying to dig a hole so it can nest in your brain. Your mouth tastes like something could be rotting in there, and the only sound you want to hear through your ringing ears is the heavenly fizz of an Alka-Seltzer. Plus, it's Monday morning and you're late for work. Damn that DQ and its late night opening. But with a host of DJs and the best funk, indie and electro beats in town how can you resist it? Well, you simply won't. In fact you'd be there every night of the week, if it didn't close on a Tuesday.

🅒 *Sun–Mon & Wed–Thu, 10pm–3am; Fri–Sat, 9pm–4am*

Dance

Embrace Nightclub

1 Burgess Street

(0114) 278 8811

The soviet hammer–and–sickle hanging over the dance floor has gone, and has been replaced by a massive, shiny, revolving lady and some palm trees. Kingdom has undergone a face-lift and there are now five swanky new theme rooms to lose your mates in. Give everyone laser guns and Embrace would be like a surreal laser-quest. Run around Cuba, Tokyo, Russia, a New York apartment and 'beach-style' bars listening to dance anthems and buying Reefs. Win bonus points if you zap Will Mellor or someone from Hollyoaks.

🕑 *Mon & Wed–Thu, 10pm–2am; Fri, 10pm–3am; Sat, 10pm–4am*

💰 *Prices vary*

Fuzz Club

Sheffield University Students' Union, Western Bank

(0114) 222 8500

The only club night in Sheffeld to promise two live bands every week, Fuzz Club is the stuff of legend among Sheffield's indie kids. Over the years it's played host to some of today's hottest acts (The Killers, The Kooks, The Rapture, Hot Chip, Editors), and local bands know they're gaining ground when asked to perform there. From 12am to 2am the Foundry plays all the indie hits of the moment amongst some alt classics, while in Fusion all your moshing needs are met with skate-punk, metal and emo anthems. Cheap drinks too.

🕑 *Every Thu, 10pm–2am*

💰 *£4 on the door; £3.50 in advance*

Flares

2–8 Carver Street

(0114) 279 5581

With enough cheese to turn a Swiss man green with envy, Flares is everything you don't want when sober, yet crave after a few too many drinks. Sing-along classics, that even your mum no longer finds cool, will emanate from your mouth as you realise you scarily know more words to them than you thought. If the alcopops keep you entranced for long enough you might end up in some sort of conga, performing the dance moves to *Saturday Night*, or worse still, doing the *Agadoo*. It was acceptable in the 80s. Apparently.

🕑 *Tue, 8pm–2am; Wed–Thu, 9pm–2am; Fri–Sat, 9pm–3am; Sun, 9pm–1am*

💰 *Prices vary*

Hot Pants @ City Hall Ballroom

Barker's Pool, Balm Green

(0114) 233 3740

If Hot Pants took on Flares in a retro clubbing experience competition, there would be one clear winner. Once a week, the flashing disco floor comes out at the City Hall and those in the know head to the heart of the city to strut their funky stuff to the likes of Blondie, Abba and the Jackson Five. There's one room dedicated to 70s, whilst the other is all about the 80s, so whatever your decade of preference is, you can find something to suit. Best to buy your ticket in advance though. Not only is it cheaper this way, but you'll also avoid the massive queue that builds up outside.

🕑 *Sat, 10pm–2am*

💰 *£6 online*

The Leadmill

6–7 Leadmill Road

(0114) 221 2828

The Leadmill holds a special place in the heart of Sheffield (well, right next to the train station in a run-down industrialised part of the centre). For over a quarter of a century the venue has been the best place in Sheffield for live music and alternative club nights, which is why people still flock here five nights a week to be taught a lesson by this granddaddy of rock music. Although the place looks its age, the bar is cheap, the dance floor is full and the music is always good.

⊕ *Fri, Sat & Mon, 10pm–2.30am;*
Wed, 10.30pm–2am; Thu, 10pm–2am
⊟ *Fri-Sat, £5 before 12am; Mon,*
Wed & Thu, £4

The Tuesday Club @ Fusion & Foundry

Sheffield University Student's Union, Western Bank

(0114) 222 8777

According to the nursery rhyme, Monday's child is fair of face. Tuesday's child is full of grace. And also enjoys a bit of a rave if the crowd at The Tuesday Club are anything to go by. Sheffield Union's excellent hip-hop and drum 'n' bass club night is the place to be seen midweek, offering a refreshing alternative to those clubs pumping out the same old 'tried and tested' playlists. It's no wonder that Wednesday's child is full of woe when they wake up with a killer hangover and have to wait another whole week to get their Tuesday Club fix.

⊕ *Tue, 10.30pm–2.30am*
⊟ *£5 on the door; £4 in advance*

Vibe

40 Charter Square

(0114) 273 8323

Want a club where you can dance your cares away and not feel like your life is in danger if you tread on somebody's toes? Best stay away from here then. Formerly known as Niche, its clientele used to have a reputation for getting as trashed as possible and then causing a lot of trouble. So the owners changed the name, spruced up the décor and whacked up the prices. But the people still act the same. We will get off our high OAP horse for just a minute to inform you that the dance music here is pretty good and it often stays open later than other clubs. But if you value your life, it's probably best to stay away.

⊕ *Times and prices vary*

Gay

Drag Kings: A Very British Affair

MEN WHO DRESS AS WOMEN ARE OLD HAT. ITCHY'S MUCH MORE OF A FAN OF THE NATION'S NEWEST GAY CRAZE – WOMEN DRESSING AS MEN. MOVE OVER DRAG QUEENS: HERE COME DRAG KINGS

Following its brief moment in the spotlight during Victorian music hall performances, drag king shows – where women dress as men – may have pretty much vanished, but they're just about to make a comeback.

Some king performers take on realistic male personas on the stage by strapping down the chest area, 'packing' (typically created by sock-filled condoms), and adding realistic facial hair. Performances are usually mimed comic songs, performed as a 'troupe' of band members. However, solo performers, who take the act into wilder and more feisty territory, are becoming increasingly common.

Worldwide, 'kinging' has moved on from the days of old, but backward Britannia is still dragging her high heels. Drag queens have long been accepted in the gay scene, and more recently in mainstream entertainment, but sadly drag kings are yet to gain the same widespread popularity.

Illustration by Si Clarke

There is some hope though. The annual Transfabulous Festival is a big showcase for drag kings, and the Wotever World group hosts a variety of different drag king-packed nights. If this risqué revolution does take hold, we reckon there's no reason drag kings shouldn't have as much stage-space as their long-successful queen counterparts. Perhaps the art of female cross-dressing is about to come home...

BARS

Affinity

29–31 Campo Lane
(07783) 197 954

Fans of the Lion's Lair please be seated for what you are about to read... the Lion's Lair is no more. But, before you give way to banshee-like wailing control yourself as there is hope – there is Affinity. Acting as the replacement pre-Fuel bar, Affinity promises to be everything the Lion's Lair was and more. Billed as a 'metrosexual' bar, anybody laid back and up for a laugh will fit in just fine. With certain drinks starting at 99p you'll be up there giving Raunchy Rusty a run for her money.
Ⓞ *Sun–Thu, 5pm–12am;*
Fri–Sat, 5pm–1am

Out @ The Raynor Lounge

Sheffield University Students' Union, Western Bank
(0114) 222 8500

The LGBT executive have come up with the bright idea of running this night right after their monthly meetings. This means you not only get to meet like-minded people, you also get to enter into a completely drunken stupor with them. All in the name of 'getting to know each other better', of course. You'll feel that warm and fuzzy feeling growing inside as you're bopping away with your new best mate, whose name you can't remember, even though you have a vague idea that it's Steve or something. And with student prices at the bar you'll even get the tequilas in.
Ⓞ *Monthly, Tue, 9pm–2am*
Ⓐ *£2 in advance; £3 on the door*

Dempsey's

1 Hereford Street
(0114) 275 4616

Hidden away in the beautiful part of the city centre named The Moor (there's irony in our voice there), Sheffield's most well-known gay establishment is just like Marmite (in the love-it-or-loathe-it sense). A little unsure of its own identity, this poor lil' venue doesn't know whether to act as a bar, restaurant or nightclub, so it tries to be all three at the same time. Itchy likes Dempsey's like Itchy likes Marmite. And with a George Michael/Duran Duran loop on the screens downstairs, as well as a tiddly dance floor the size of a parking space upstairs, what more could you ask for? Not much at all from Dempsey's.
Ⓞ *Sun–Thu, 12pm–3am; Fri–Sat, 12pm–4am*

Roebuck Tavern

72 Charles Street
(0114) 272 1756

While this pub is not strictly a gay venue, it is gay-friendly, and given the slightly limited choice that Sheffield offers it serves as another option. That's if you want the option of a place that has the slight aroma and feel of an old man's pub to it. Still, in a bid to drag their pub kicking and screaming into the 21st century, they've only gone and added a PlayStation 2 with free use (although Itchy think we'd all agree that a PS3 would now be nice. Or a Wii, although coupled with alcohol, that could end messily). Not the trendiest place in town, but it'll do for a pint or two.
Ⓞ *Sun–Thu, 11am–11pm; Fri, 11am–12.30am; Sat, 11am–12am*

Gay

CLUBS

Climax @ Fusion & Foundry

Sheffield University Students' Union, Western Bank

(0114) 222 8500

Fuel may hold the throne as the queen of gay clubs in Sheffield, but every month this night gives it a good fight for the crown. Camper than a Scout jamboree, Climax is South Yorkshire's premier LGB clubbing experience. Pole dancers, glitterballs and a soundsystem pumping out all of your favourite club anthems. So get out your tiaras, wands, skinny tees, glo-sticks, feather boas, sparkly bits etc., and prepare yourself for the most outrageous night you've had in ages.

🕐 *Monthly (on a Friday), 10pm–3am*

🎟 *£4.50 in advance; £5 on the door*

Club Xes

195 Carlisle Street, Attercliffe

(0114) 275 0828

Do you want the good news or the bad news first? Ok, well the good news is that this is a marvellously refreshing gay venue that manages to keep the students at bay, so it's purely adult entertainment. The bad news is that it's in Attercliffe, dun dun duuuunn. Alright so it's not that bad but it will require a taxi ride from town. And here comes that good news again, its late opening means you can pop along there once your regular hangout has shut. Perfick.

🕐 *Wed–Thu, 10pm–4am; Fri–Sat, 9pm–5am; Sun, 9pm–3am*

🎟 *Wed, free; Thu, £1; Fri–Sat, £3 after 11pm; Sun, £1*

Fuel @ Red Room

25–33 Carter Street

(0114) 263 4264

Every Saturday night, come 10.30pm the Red Room transforms into a haven for the extravagant as Sheffield's favourite gay venue moves in. Now poor Fuel has had a tough time recently settling into different premises since the end of its love affair with Plug, but hopefully now it has finally found a place it can call home. If you're up for a riotous sort of a time, a bit of dancing with some gorgeous drag queens and generally a fabulous glitzy night then Fuel will not disappoint. A night out here will leave you feeling happier than Santa on Valium. And probably less likely to do for yourself in a sledging accident.

🕐 *Sat, 10.30pm–3am*

OTHER

Brockett House

1 Montgomery Road
(0114) 258 8952

Exclusively for gay and lesbian travellers, this guesthouse offers a little something special. Built in 1873 and located in the leafy Victorian area of Nether Edge, it could be your very own escape. You might end up feeling a little Mr Darcy, (not literally we're sorry to say). Or if that's not your thing, why not act all David Beckham-like and borrow one of the hotel's sarongs to saunter around your room in? The management not only allow sarong-sauntering, they actively encourage it. Whatever happened to mere complimentary towels, eh?

🏠 *Room rates vary*

Out Aloud – Sheffield's Gay Choir

(07982) 896 806

Fancy yourself as the next Michael Jackson or Britney Spears? Well your aspirations don't seem to be very high then. If, on the other hand, you'd like to learn how to sing well, get yourself along to Out Aloud. The good thing is that you don't have to have sung before or know how to read music. So just like Whoopi Goldberg's lot in *Sister Act*, you could enter being awful and come out winning competitions. With the rehearsals being described as 'fun and uplifting' how could you not be tempted? So go on, fill your lungs, raise your arms and belt out a good 'un.

🕐 *Rehearsals every Wed, 7.15pm–9.30pm*

Bronx Sauna

208 Saville Street East
(0114) 278 6440

Fancy getting all hot and sweaty, or perhaps a bit steamy, followed by that bubbly feeling all over your skin? And no, we're not talking about your first date with that chap you pulled the other night when you had your maximum-strength beer goggles on. We're talking saunas, and this one is top of our list. If you like the sound of warming up in a steam room, splashing about in a Jacuzzi, or just relaxing in a solarium and doing all this in a gay-friendly environment, then why don't you treat yourself? Just make sure you don't bump into that pull in the steam room...

🕐 *Mon–Thu, 11am–11pm; Sat, 1pm–6am*

Shop

Shop

Welcome to Shop

Meadowhall may have stolen all the good chain stores from the city centre, but there's still plenty of fun to be had away from that beast of a shopping centre. Bit of a raver? Shake your booty down to **Studio Beatz (159 West Street, 0114 273 9107)**. Or if you're a bit of a bargain hunter then take a wander around **The Moor Markets (The Moor)**, or you could head to **Freshmans (6–8 Carver Street, 0114 272 8333)**, with its eclectic clothing collections and funky retro accessories. If you find Freshmans a bit too random for your poor little head, but you don't want to lose your rep with the cool kids then cross over the road to **Ark (1–3 Devonshire Street, 0114 272 2561)**. In fact, there's so many great shops around, we can guarantee your hands won't be empty when you leave. But your bank account certainly will.

Top five bits of tourist tat to buy in Sheffield

A spoon, knife or fork – You're in the steel city, so it has to be done.

100 clothes pegs – Or something equally useless from the market.

A bottle of Henderson's Relish Our answer to Worcester sauce.

A loyalty card from the pub Because every boozer has one.

Sheffield United/Sheffield Wednesday football shirt Choose your side… either way you will be heckled.

Top five shops to bag a bargain in

Freshmans – Look like an indie-pop star, for a fraction of the price.

Moor Markets – Pretty much everything costs less than £1.

Cancer Research – The best excuse to shop: for a good cause.

Rare and Racy – Browse the shelves for that one-off that'll make you rich when you sell it on eBay.

Evolution – Kit your whole house out and still expect change for a fiver in their sales.

MARKETS

The Moor Markets

The Moor

A thousand batteries for a pound, genuine-ish designer underwear for cheaper than charity shop y-fronts, and the name of your football team on absolutely anything you can think of – this is the pedestrianised personification of *Only Fools & Horses*. From what seems like the world's largest selection of Pick 'n' Mix to stuff that's been recently nicked, take a fiver, explore for hours, and then postulate upon a) how long your goods might last before disintegrating, and b) what the hell you might do with ten bath towels, a feather duster and a set of Derby County-themed dinnerware.

SHOPPING CENTRES

Meadowhall

1 the Oasis, Meadowhall Centre

(0114) 256 8800

Meadowhall appears to operate in some parallel universe; you feel like you've been in there for half an hour yet mysteriously three hours of your life have gone and you haven't purchased a thing. Having realised you've suddenly lost all sense of direction and finding that the one shop that you went there for must have closed down, you eventually stumble out. It may not be easy going, but with its 9pm closing, it's just magic for picking out a last-minute present for your mum's birthday that she'll return the week after.

Ⓒ *Mon–Fri, 10am–9pm; Sat, 9am–7pm; Sun, 11am–5pm*

Shop

MUSIC

Studio Beatz

159 West Street

(0114) 273 9107

If Itchy owned a record store, we'd have a lot of fun bamboozling unsuspecting punters. 'Alright mate. Yeah this one's brand new. It used to be a sub-Latin-electro-jazz-dub-hard-drum-and-bass tune featuring vocals from Pavarotti. It's been given an electro house remix by Pierre Le Club and on the other side it's got a rare unreleased rap song about Walkers crisps by David Beckham.' Luckily for you, we don't own Studio Beatz, which stocks a good selection of house and garage on vinyl, as well as other DJ gear.

🕓 *Mon–Sat, 10am–6pm*

WOMEN'S CLOTHING

Alice Takes a Trip

127–129 Devonshire Street

(0114) 272 0946

The Forum Shops are pretty much the rum at the heart of the mojito giving old Sheffield the extra kick it needs. And if you lost us in metaphor there, we meant they're cool and saucy. And Alice Takes a Trip is the coolest. Alice provides all the retro, vintage fashion you could ever need to feel as boho chic as Sienna Miller and Kate Moss all rolled into one. On the downside, they make no guarantee you will snag yourself a Jude Law-alike, but hey, it also means you won't be stuck with a Pete Crackerty-alike either.

🕓 *Mon–Sat, 10am–6pm; Sun, 11am–5pm*

Republic

12–13 High Street, Meadowhall Shopping Centre

(0114) 256 9143

'Join the republic' is their frankly slightly uninspired motto, but with the tasty range of brands these guys keep in stock, we definitely want to be their comrades in fashion-arms. Specialising in funky brands like Firetrap, those less cool might be a little scared to enter the land of the free (or in this case the über-trendy). Not us though, we're ready to sign on the dotted line, and though our wallets might not be able to handle it, we know our stylish bodies will. There are two levels to this magical shop, which means buckle up, this could be a long ride.

🕓 *Mon–Fri, 10am–9pm; Sat, 9am–7pm; Sun, 11am–5pm*

UNISEX CLOTHING

Ark

114 Devonshire Street

(0114) 272 2561

For some new threads for a special occasion or that must-have hat/belt/scarf, then Ark is the place to visit. They stock a selection of clothes from the likes of Bench, Superdry and the Doherty and Winehouse endorsed Gio-Goi. You can enhance your rock-star credentials without hassle by simply buying a T-shirt that proclaims to stalking paparazzi that you are 'drug-free', thus making them uninterested in you. You won't need to fall out of a taxi, or find yourself a supermodel girlfriend to feel like you're living the dream here.

● *Mon–Sat, 10am–6pm; Sun, 11am–4.30pm*

Envy

720 High Street, Lower Mall, Meadowhall

(0114) 256 8647

Here at Itchy we're all in favour of designer gear. And yes, that includes the stuff you get from the market that looks nearly the same. However, the clothes at Envy don't really make us green with, well, you know. They've got some decent stuff. Boxfresh does ok jumpers to buy for Christmas presents, but us stylised scenesters just aren't really feeling the Playboy collection anymore. Envy needs to update its stock to keep with its ever-cool clientele, like us trendsetters at Itchy HQ. Little pink bunny bags will just no longer be on our shopping wish lists.

● *Mon–Fri, 10am–9pm; Sat, 10am–7pm; Sun, 11am–5pm*

Bench

73 High Street, Meadowhall Shopping Centre

(0114) 256 8292

Like some surreal urban version of the house on *Finders Keepers*, the UK's only store dedicated exclusively to Bench clothing is an attraction all in itself. Once you get over Bench's slightly unnerving fascination with toilets (Itchy spotted four, see how many you can find), head towards the back of the shop to try on clothes onboard an underground train replica. You can even experience life as a store mannequin, as a picture of your face is placed above the dummies in the window. Oh, and the clothes aren't too bad either, which is always a bonus for a clothes shop.

● *Mon–Fri, 10am–9pm; Sat, 9am–7pm; Sun, 11am–5pm*

Fat Face

7 Orchard Square

(0114) 279 8635

Oddly enough, this isn't a shop dedicated to Michelle McManus. Besides, surely that would just be called, 'Fat Person'. Fat Face caters for all the 'gnarly' types among you. Whether you want an outfit for the slopes or one for the beach, this shop has all you need to ensure you look cool whatever your environment. Clothes from here should withstand minor bumps and scrapes if you're an action-packed adrenaline junkie. They're also good for making you look like you're into extreme sports when actually the most activity you have in a day is getting up to turn the TV over when the remote's broken.

● *Mon–Sat, 9am–5.30pm; Sun, 11am–5pm*

Shop

River Island

58–64 Fargate, Orchard Square

(0114) 273 8607

One of the first things to strike you about this store is the abundance of sequins, leopard print and ruffled material. And that's just the staff in menswear. As a relatively new store, Sheffield's River Island has pulled out all the stops to be the biggest, brashest fashion store on the high street. If the neon signs and bright lighting don't blind you first, you may have a chance to look at the clothes on offer. Among all the glitter and thigh-skimming skirts, there are some tasty designer rip-offs to be found and, although it ain't no Primark, the prices aren't too bad really.

◉ *Mon–Fri, 9am–5pm; Sat, 9am–6pm; Sun, 11am–5pm*

USC

11 Fargate

(0114) 275 0052

USC is like one of those 'backup' friends you might have. You'd never allocate your Saturday night to them straight off, just in case something more exciting came along, but you'd be on the phone to them like a shot if you found out that your other plans were going to fall through. Thus it is with USC. You wouldn't go in there first thing, mostly because the prices are too high and Diesel is just so 2004, dahling. You would, however, have a good long search through a whole heap of other shops and, having not found that perfect top, end up trying and succeeding in USC. It's a shopper's safety net.

◉ *Mon–Fri, 9.30am–6pm; Sat, 9am–6pm*

SECONDHAND

Bullet

275 Sharrowvale Road

(0114) 267 6665

So, Starsky and Hutch stumble across a time machine, stupidly get in it and manage to transport themselves into Sheffield circa now. What in the blue blazes do they do? Well, after sampling the delights of a post-millennium lifestyle and failing to see the advantages of modern living, they might head to Bullet. Dripping with furniture, glassware, even bars, from the 70s and beyond, the two careless detectives would most definitely pick themselves up a few treats. In fact, why not join them?

◉ *Wed & Fri–Sat, 10.30am–6pm or by appointment*

Freshmans Boutique

6–8 Carver Street

(0114) 272 8333

Is your wardrobe in desperate need of a rainbow-coloured curly wig? Or a bright blue Hawaiian print shirt? What about a silver puffball dress? If you're lacking in these and other such fashion essentials, get down to Freshmans Boutique. Ideal for both fancy dress and unique everyday items, the owner trawls round America, looking for the very best in secondhand retro wear so the people of Sheffield can look über cool. It's just like a well-stocked, fashion-conscious charity shop, but the people behind the till are younger and hotter and there are not quite so many hand-knitted Christmas jumpers on the shelves.

◉ *Mon–Sat, 10am–6pm; Sun, 11.30am–5pm*

Cancer Research Charity Shop

411 Ecclesall Road

(0114) 267 9150

Rumoured to benefit from links with the Meadowhall Lost and Found Department, the Cancer Research shop provides exceptional services to any students whose shoestring budgets have started to fray. Those who shuffle in nervously will be happy to find a charity shop that consistently offers some brilliant bargains, without too much debris to hamper your rummaging. Not to say that other thrift stores in the area aren't worth a look – you're going to have to work hard if you want to find that copy of Toploader's second album.

◉ *Mon–Sat, 9.30am–5.30pm; occasional Sundays, 1pm–5.30pm*

Shop

Rare & Race

164–166 Devonshire Street

(0114) 270 1916

A bit like the bookshop in George Orwell's *Keep the Aspidistra Flying* – what? Too intellectual? Then you should definitely come here and read up on your literature, history and just about everything you can get your hands on to transform you into a witty, reference-dropping smart-arse. Like an Aladdin's cave for readers, this place is stacked from floor to ceiling with books. And for those of you who aren't too keen on the art of reading, it also has a similar amount of records too. A fantastic place to go and get yourself lost in for a few hours; you may come out a bit dusty, but you're sure to have found your own bit of treasure.

◉ *Mon–Sat, 10am–5pm*

The Parlour Room

300 Sharrowvale Road

(0114) 268 6374

Remember that programme *Goodnight Sweetheart* with Rodney from *Only Fools and Horses*? He'd walk through a wall and end up in the 1940s. Well, when you walk through the door of this shop, that's exactly what happens. Well, not exactly. You don't suddenly find yourself fighting the Nazis in Stalingrad or swimming around in Pearl Harbour, obviously, but you are suddenly surrounded by enough memorabilia from yesteryear to make you think you've just accomplished the art of time travel. Pick yourself up some war medals, sheet music or a frilly underskirt; whatever floats your antique boat.

◉ *Wed, 11am–7pm; Sat, 10am–5.30pm*

OTHER

Design Studio

417–419 Ecclesall Road
(0114) 268 3033

What do you buy the person who has everything? Frankly, we don't think you should buy them anything, the greedy sods. But if you're having one of those Mother Teresa days, you could stop by here and see if something tickles your fancy. A bit of jewellery perhaps? Or a hand-made card that costs as much as a diamond-encrusted ring? Or some other novelty gift? Nobody needs what this shop sells, but then again, we're all entitled to a bit of pointless yet sparkly extravagance now and again.

🕙 *Mon–Sat, 9.30am–6pm; Sun, 12pm–5pm*

Mookau

391 Ecclesall Road
(0114) 266 8994

Another addition to the selection of spangly boutiques on Ecclesall Road that doesn't really sell anything of particular use, unless sparkly hanging letters count. That said, Mookau does provide dozens of last-minute present ideas, from furry telephones and miniature ping-pong tables, to designer espresso cups and more candles than you could shake a hoof at. An aluminium-cast 'beer money' box may appeal perfectly to the student crowd, but at £20 it seems you'd probably have precious little left to put in it. Still, looking at those sparkly letters might hypnotise you...

🕙 *Mon–Sat, 10am–6.30pm; Sun, 11am–5pm*

Evolution

9 Orchard Square
(0114) 276 8766

Once again, you've left buying your mate's birthday pressie to the last minute, and have no idea what to buy. Well, as Evolution knows, you can't really go far wrong with picture frames, candles and mirrors. This place is also good if you wanted to pretend that you've just finished a gap year. Nip in and buy a tribal mask or a statue of Buddha. No one need know that you holiday in Zante. Feel good while shopping too because Evolution is run by Buddhists. It tries to be environmentally friendly and ensures foreign goods are made under ethical conditions.

🕙 *Mon, 10am–5.30pm; Tue–Sat, 9.30am–5.30pm; Sun, 11am–5pm*

Shop

Mr Ben's Fancy Dress

170 Crookes

(0114) 266 6470

'Arr, here lies treasure, me hearties. I hears, with me one good ear, that this is the place to dig for fancy dress gold. Beware! You may enter 'ere in search of one thing but you'll probably leave with something other. Many of me mateys have got themselves battle scars here (albeit fake ones, it's amazing how real plastic wounds look). Legend also has it that them tharr Arctic Monkeys found their costumes here before they went to pick up their Brit awards.' Impressed by our pirate impersonation? Us neither. Head down to Mr Ben's to transform yourself into something far more convincing (bad pirate accent not included).

⏰ Mon–Fri, 10am–6pm; Sat, 10am–5pm

Within Reason

144–146 Devonshire Street

(0114) 249 3346

Sugar and spice and all things nice – that's what this shop is made of. If you like your furniture to be pretty and your accessories to sparkle and your general knick-knacks to be quirky then this shop is right up your street. Deck your house with boughs of holly, tra la la la la la... etc., but when it's not time for Christmas cheer, come here to stock up on an assortment of treasures to keep the spirit going all year long; it'll look like Cinderella's marvellous fairy godmother has had her wand waving around your humble abode. It's also a good place to pick up a few prezzies for your mates – they'll think you're pretty magical too.

⏰ Mon–Sat, 10am–5.30pm

Williamson Hardware

222 Fulwood Road

(0114) 266 1911

Buying diverse items in a hardware store is right up in the top ten of Macho Things You Can Do. It ranks alongside other classic manly pursuits like using power tools, downing pints, chopping wood, opening jars, driving minibuses, carving roast dinners, nodding at policemen, sharpening pencils with a knife and calling everyone 'son'. It doesn't matter if you actually have any aptitude for DIY, just go in the store, swing a few hammers about and pose in front of the mirror brandishing an orbital sander. Grrrrrr, reckon this bad boy should do the job, son. Four candles? We asked for fork handles...

⏰ Mon–Fri, 9am–5pm; Sat, 10am–4.30pm

Out & About

Out & About

Welcome to Out & About

Sheffield may feel like a village but it is in fact the fourth largest city in the land, so there's loads of ways to kill your time here. **The Last Laugh Comedy Club (Memorial Hall, Barkers Pool, 0114 223 3752)** is a great if you like a few tipples and a bit of a giggle. But if it takes a lot more than a bit of comedy to really thrill you, then head for the **Magna Science Adventure Centre (Sheffield Road, Rotheram, 01709 720 002)**. They have the UK's only indoor bungee jump and the old steel works setting means this comes with an adrenaline pumping guarantee. For those of a slightly gentler disposition, **The Winter Gardens (Surrey Street, 0114 221 1900)** is the must-see attraction. You can't say you've been to Sheffield if you haven't been inside the giant's greenhouse. And if that whets your cultural appetite, then get over to **Weston Park Museum (Western Bank, 0114 278 2600)**, where you can learn all about the history of Sheffield, from the ice age to World War II.

Top five summer activities

Peak District – Don't forget the walking boots.

Weston Park Museum – Laze in the park 'til it rains, then hop inside.

Chatsworth House – Pretend you're in a Jane Austen novel.

Botanical Gardens – Peace, tranquillity and ice cream for all.

Metrodome Water Park – British summers suck, so go to Barnsley and pretend you're in Hawaii.

Top five winter activities

Magna Science Park– It may be out of the wind and rain, but it's still freezing, so take a jumper.

Winter Gardens – Like a little bit of summer got left behind.

Panto at the Lyceum – Great fun. Oh, no it's not... Oh yes it is.

Last Laugh Comedy Club – Warm those cockles with a good giggle.

Ice Sheffield – Because ice-skating just doesn't feel right in the summer.

Local Band Pubs *Dahling!*

AFTER THE RECENT SUCCESS OF BANDS LIKE THE ARCTIC MONKEYS, REVEREND AND THE MAKERS, HARRISONS AND THE LONG BLONDES, AND WITH THE BACK CATALOGUE OF SHEFFIELD'S MUSIC SCENE INCLUDING THE LIKES OF PULP, DEF LEPPARD AND THE HUMAN LEAGUE, EVERY PUB WANTS TO BE ABLE TO BOAST THAT THEY WERE FIRST TO BRING YOU THE NEXT BIG THING....

There is actually a plaque in Hallam University which marks where the Human League first performed live. Such an enthusiastic attitude to new music makes Sheffield a fertile breeding ground of talent (look out for the likes of Monkey Swallows, The Universe, Slow Down Tallahasses and many of the other bands that are part of the Sheffield Phonographic Corporation). While it is true that pub bands, even ones from Sheffield, can sometimes be a bit hit and miss, the **Frog and Parrot (Division Street, 0114 272 1280)** has more of the former and less of the latter. Check out their brilliant 'Frogstock' mini-festival to get your fill of local talent (and cheap ale). Their pub grub is pretty fine too. But back on the band trail, you'll find **The Green Room (150–154 Devonshire Street, 0114 249 3329)** just round the corner, which is well noted for its acoustic sets from the likes of local folk favourites Slow Club, and chilled out jazz sessions. If you prefer funky basslines and music you can really move your feet to, then carry on down Division Street and keep walking until you get to Glossop Road, where **The Harley (334 Glossop Road, 0114 275 2288)** stands proud. This down and dirty pub showcases the best of the best every Monday, and – it gets better – it's all completely free. What's that you say? Still not heavy enough for you? If you really like music that makes your ears bleed head to the **Dove and Rainbow (Hartshead Square, 0114 272 1594)**. Yes, it sounds like a gay bar, but its speciality is rock music and its ethos is 'the heavier the better'. If you can't find 'the next big thing' in any of these places then we suggest you get your ears tested.

Out & About

CINEMAS

Odeon Cinema

Arundel Gate

(0114) 224 3981

There's one thing about Odeon cinemas which baffles us: the fact that after the adverts and trailers have been shown, the lights in the room suddenly come on and the curtains close across the screen. Now this may have been fine in the days when there was a nice lady selling ice creams from a tray hanging around her neck, but without this luxury, this weirdly brief interval isn't such a welcome interruption. You'll probably fill the time by eating all your popcorn, meaning you'll have none left by the time the film actually starts.

From 11am; last viewing, 9pm

UGC Cineworld

Valley Centertainment, Broughton Lane

(0870) 902 0420

With a gob-smacking 20 screens and a complex system of swivelling doors, escalators and corridors, it's amazing that anybody who enters this Cineworld actually manages to find their way out again. You can guarantee that they'll be showing the latest Hollywood release at least six times a day, and if you're willing to hand over an extortionate amount of money, there are plenty of fat-filled snacks for you to choose from. Like our mate's rugby-playing ex-boyfriend, what it has in size, it lacks in personality. But then what can you expect when it's situated in a place called Centertainment?

Mon–Sun, 9am–9pm

The Showroom

7 Paternoster Row

(0114) 275 7727

If you thought unemployed steel workers wiggling their bits in front of ravenous post-menopausal women was as high-brow as cinema gets in Sheffield, then think again. The Showroom is one of the most prestigious cinemas in the country, hosting documentaries, film festivals and even movies with subtitles. Don't worry though, it's not full of beret-wearing artistic types all day, as the latest commercial blockbuster will also make an appearance. So you can sneak in pretending to be all arty-farty but actually grab a bucket of popcorn and a seat a in front of the newest gore-fest.

Sun–Thu, 1pm–9pm;
Fri–Sat, 1pm–10.30pm

COMEDY

Last Laugh Comedy Club @ The Lescar

303 Sharrow Vale Road

(0114) 267 9787

If you feel like a good old belly roar then this is the place to go. A back room in a backstreet pub may not seem like the obvious bet for an evening of non-stop funnies, but appearances can be deceiving, don't you know. The likes of Jimmy Carr and Peter Kay have performed here, albeit when they weren't famous, but that's not the point. The comedy stars of the future could be just a few feet in front of you.

Ⓒ *Every Thursday; doors, 8pm; show, 8.30pm*

Ⓐ £7

THEATRE

Lyceum Theatre

55 Norfolk Street

(0114) 249 6000

The Crucible (the Lyceum's younger, better-looking sister) may get all the classy, cutting-edge performances but every Sheffielder knows that the real fun is to be had at the Lyceum. Playing host to all the West End shows that London has already chewed up and spat out, you can find musicals, camp comedy acts and seasonal soap star-studded pantos galore in this wonderfully decadent theatre (we'll have none of this minimalist rubbish here). Who needs *Doctor Faustus* when you can see *Puppetry of the Penis* just next door?

Ⓒ *Shows, 7.30pm; some matinees*

LIVE MUSIC

Hallam FM Arena

Broughton Lane

(0114) 256 5656

Some big names have played at the arena: Take That, Stereophonics, Michael Bublé (well we did say *some* big names) so it's the place to keep your eye on if you want to catch your favourite artist. Plus it's bloomin' massive inside, with tiered seating so you don't have to worry about getting a big head or ludicrous novelty hat sat slap bang in front of you. Also home to sports such as basketball, ice hockey and boxing, as well as an annual fireworks display on Bonfire Night, it's not just music lovers who'll find something to like here.

Ⓒ *Times and prices vary*

Out & About

MUSEUMS

Chatsworth House
Bakewell, Derbyshire
(01246) 565 300

We're not ones to turn our noses up at a place. Certainly not. And if this stately home was good enough for Mr Darcy and Elizabeth Bennet (it was used as a location in the film *Pride and Prejudice*), then it's good enough for us. Landscaped gardens with a big old beautiful house plonked in the middle, what more could one ask for? This place is simply spiffing, although it may make you feel like your own humble abode is a little cramped and shoddily furnished when you get home. Cheers Ikea.

◉ *Mon–Sun, house, 11am–5.30pm; gardens, 11am–6pm*

Kelham Island Museum
Alma Street
(0114) 272 2106

Ah, the story of our lady Sheffield – now we'll be the first to admit that this might not be exactly the most crowd-pleasing and high octane of the Steel City's attractions, but a little bit of historical knowledge goes a long way. Well, that's what our teachers always used to tell us back in the day, and look where it got us here at Itchy. If nothing else it should at least provide you with some great pub quiz ammunition. So, go on, take a look around. Rise above the jibes of the hypocrites and appreciate how good it is to feel wise.

◉ *Mon–Thu, 10am–4pm; Sun, 11am–4.45pm*

🅰 £4

Fire & Police Museum
West Bar
(0114) 249 1999

London's Burning or *The Bill*? *Fireman Sam* or... well, there is no policeman children's character so maybe Sam wins that one by default. Still, if you're musing over which job is the best, perhaps this is the place to give you the answer and settle that pub argument. Memorabilia from both professions is in abundance at the volunteer-run museum, but with appearances from Sam the man himself and fire engine rides, we at Itchy think the police might just be pipped at the post by the boys in the big red trucks.

◉ *Sundays and Bank Holiday Mondays, 11am–5pm*

🅰 £4

Magna Science Adventure Centre
Sheffield Road, Rotherham
(01709) 720 002

Sounds exciting, eh? And so it damn well should. With its four pavilions allowing you to travel through air, earth, fire and water, you'll go where no man has ever gone before (unless they've already visited Magna, of course). Just when you thought it wasn't possible, the centre manages to make learning fun. So we say 'pish' to those who reckon you can't teach an old dog new tricks – you'll be lapping up info left, right and centre. Oh, and take a hint from the name of the 'Aqua-Tek' playground: you will need waterproofs.

◉ *Mon–Sun, 10am–5pm*

🅰 £9.95; concs, £7.97

Western Park Museum
Western Bank
(0114) 278 2600

This is one of those please-the-whole-family places. We're not complaining though. Sometimes even us ever-so-cool types here at Itchy like to have a day out feeling and, well, acting, like kids. Western Park has light shows, hands-on interactive displays, and historical relics that are actually interesting to look at. The Egyptian mummies are just part of the adventure. Yeah, we know what we sound like and we just don't care. You won't either after you've spent the day exploring the wonders of the world from our very own Sheffield museum.

🕙 *Mon–Sat, 10am–5pm; Sun, 11am–5pm*
🎫 *Free*

GALLERIES

Graves Art Gallery
Surrey Street
(0114) 278 2600

Shhhh. Don't speak too loudly in here. Scrap that. Don't even cough too loudly in here, and certainly don't wear squeaky shoes or those wheely light trainers the kids are sporting. Art galleries are quiet at the best of times, but an art gallery above a library is a place more silent than a convent when all the nuns are huddled round a sneaky portable watching *Father Ted*. Permanent displays of modern art happily share their wall space with collections that are simply passing through.

🕙 *Mon–Sat, 10am–5pm*
🎫 *Free*

Out & About

Millennium Galleries

Arundel Gate

(0114) 278 2600

A big monster made out of spoons and forks that makes a noise when you press a button? What more could you want? And guess what one of the gallery's crowning exhibitions is? We'll give you a clue: it's what the steel city is famous for. That's right folks, metal work. From old spoons to a big punch bowl, this room has it all. With special exhibitions, a novel gift shop and connection to the Winter Gardens, it's the ideal place when you're forced to take visiting family around Sheffield's attractions.

🕑 *Mon–Sat, 8am–5pm (exhibitions from 10am); Sun, 11am–5pm*

🎫 *Free entry to Millennium Galleries; varying charges for special exhibitions*

PARKS

Peak District National Park

Aldern House, Baslow Road

(01626) 981 3227

Due to the popularity of games such as *Guitar Hero*, *Singstar*, and *Pro-Evo*, there seems to be no need for anybody to experience fresh air or real life anymore. However, until somebody invents a game for the Nintendo Wii called *Virtual National Park*, there isn't any way to get windswept without actually physically getting off the sofa and going in search of a hill. The Peak District is only a brief bus ride away and you can go cycling, walking, climbing, caving, sailing, windsurfing and, erm... well dressing, (we would go further and recommend this last).

Rother Valley Country Park

Mansfield Road

(0114) 247 1452

Three words for you: cable, water and ski. Oh yes, the revolution is here, and Rother Valley Park has it. Water skiing without the need of a boat. Absolutely bloody genius. If you're one of these adventurous types then get yourself on some skis, grab hold of the cable and watch as your life, (we mean the lake), whizzes past your eyes. You yellow-bellied ones can simply stand and gawp in admiration at this wondrous water sport. Oh yeah, there's also play areas and grass and stuff for those of you who like that sort of thing. Go on if you want, we won't think any less of you.

🕑 *Mon–Sun, 9am–5pm (winter season, Oct–Mar); 9am–8pm (summer season)*

SPORT

Goodwin Sports Centre

132 Northumberland Road

(0114) 222 6958

With so much time on their hands, you can find students enjoying a whole range of sports and activities at the University of Sheffield's sports complex. But fear not, fellow taxpayers, you too can enjoy all of Goodwin's facilities. From the swimming pool to the climbing wall, via yoga classes and archery, whether you want to take up something new, or continue your favourite sport, there is something for everyone. Itchy's favourite activity has to be steaming in the steam room.

☻ *Mon–Fri, 9am–10pm; Sat–Sun, 9am–5pm*

🍴 *Swimming, £3.50*

Owlerton Dog Racing

Owlerton Stadium Penistone Road

(0114) 2343074

Apparently the stadium had a £3 million facelift in 1991 and it's probably safe to say it hasn't had a thing done to it since. The toilets are not the nicest environment, even considering that their main purpose is to house piss and shit. The wine will also leave you with an unsavoury taste in your mouth, so best take it with you on your bathroom breaks. All this aside, even if you're a prissy princess you'll still have a bloody good time. Before you know it you'll be jumping up and down screaming at the bloke next to him, demanding to know which dog won. Good luck.

☻ *Race days: Tue, Fri & Sat evenings; Mon & Thu lunchtimes*

Ice Sheffield

Coleridge Road, Attercliffe

(0114) 223 3900

Cheese and ice never went so well together as they do at Ice Sheffield's discos. It's mandatory to sing along to *Ice Ice Baby* and other hilarious ice-themed song lyrics as you skate around the Olympic-sized rink, trying your best not to fall on your backside as you dodge the hand-holding couples and pint-sized speed skaters. If you really have fallen over one too many times, head to the bar upstairs where you can watch everyone else making fools of themselves while you sit smugly in the warm with your (ice cold) beverage in your hand.

☻ *Public skating session times vary*

🍴 *£4 (skate hire, £1.50)*

Ponds Forge International Sports Centre

Sheaf Street

(0114) 279 9766

Known best as the host to the reality TV show *The Games*, and home to one of the best competition pools in the country, Ponds Forge is desperate to prove itself as more than just a swimming pool. And to our great delight, it's managing to do just that. Dive further down into the very depths of Ponds Forge and you'll find the Roundhouse, a great entertainment venue, renowned for its lively atmosphere and comedy nights. Perfect if you like a laugh after a length or two.

☻ *Mon–Thu, 6.30am–10pm; Fri, 7.30am–9.30pm; Sat–Sun, 8am–9.30pm*

🍴 *Swimming pool admission, £4.10*

Out & About

PAINTBALL AND KARTING

Parkwood Karting

Parkwood Road

(0114) 279 9666

Does racing at 50 miles per hour, just inches from the ground, with nothing to protect you but a crash helmet sound like fun to you? It sure does to us. Although it's not quite that simple, there's a minimum number of participants (six, if you're asking), you have to book in advance. Then, there's the safety video to watch and the consent forms to sign. Ok, we're not doing a good job of selling this. Let's just scrap this review and just replace it with the words: 'karting = fun, fun, fun'.

◉ *Mon–Fri & Sun, 10am–9.30pm*

🎫 *Mini Grand Prix, £35 per driver*

OUTDOOR SWIMMING

King Edward VII Swimming Pool

Clarkehouse Road

(0114) 267 1116

It's probably not necessary to explain what this place is about. It is, however, worth pointing out that this is a seriously decent place to get some exercise in Sheffield, compared to our usual methods of igniting the dance floors of the city's drinking establishments. King Edward's offers aerobic classes for all ages and general swimming, as well as lessons for those who didn't have to endure being thrown into a lake and made to either swim or drown. Not that we're bitter, dad.

🎫 *General swim for adults, £4*

Skirmish Paintballing

Nursery Street

(0114) 249 3119

Don't be fooled by the fact that Skirmish Paintballing is situated in Nursery Street. It's definitely not for the under-fives. In fact, on entering the site you could be forgiven for thinking you had actually signed your life away to the MoD. Everybody stalks around in camouflage gear and masks, and makeshift camps are set out at various points around the neon paint-spattered site. But if this all seems a bit scary for you, you could always try joining one of the kiddie parties, which have specially-designed paintball guns that don't hurt nearly as much.

◉ *Times vary*

🎫 *Full day, from £10 plus cost of paintballs*

TOURIST ATTRACTIONS

Winter Gardens

Town Hall, Surrey Street

(0114) 272 6444

Sheffield has 74 parks and green spaces but who wants to go outdoors when Sheffield has its very own Eden Project? The giant greenhouse is situated in the centre of town for those rare days, ahem, when it rains in Sheffield. Check out the tropical plants when you can't enjoy watching people getting soaked in the fountains in the neighbouring Peace Gardens. It's free to get in and has an art gallery next door, the Crucible Theatre opposite and a library nearby.

◉ *Mon–Sun, 8am–6pm*

🎫 *Free*

Botanical Gardens

Clarkehouse Road

(0114) 250 0500

History? Check. Important buildings? Check. Roses, sunflowers, and daffodils? Check. Alright, we know, this might sound a little like you should be wearing Hush Puppies and one of those plastic rain bonnets, but Itchy will be the first to admit that once in a while even we need a break from the bustle of the steel city. So we go to the Botanical Gardens, because for peaceful ambience and serene settings, nothing beats this place. You might even see a wedding ceremony while you inhale the fresh air, which gets even hardcores like us a bit misty round the eyes.

☺ *Mon–Fri, 8am–7.45pm;*
Sat–Sun, 10am–7.45pm

Skate Central

Queens Road

(0114) 272 3037

Situated above the Mecca Bingo Hall, this little leisure venue was formally the Silver Blades' ice rink. Not much has changed except the name and the fact that when you fall over, your knees don't get wet. And you do fall over a lot. The plastic panels that have been laid down in the transformation tend to stick up, creating a bit of a hazard for the unobservant skater, and the wheels in your clunky skates often get jammed. But the kids seem to love it, so who are we to spoil their fun?

☺ *Tue & Thu, 6pm–9pm; Fri, 7pm–10pm;*
Sat & Sun, 2pm–4pm

☺ *Mon–Fri, £2.50 before 7pm; Mon–Fri,*
after 7pm & Sat–Sun, £3 (£1.50 skate hire)

OTHER

Hollywood Bowl

Valley Centertainment, Broughton Lane

(0114) 244 4333

Although there are 26 lanes, you're still likely to end up waiting if you haven't booked in advance. Fear not though, as there are plenty of other flashing signs and machines begging for your money. The bar and café provide you with American sustenance and the arcade area caters for all, from wannabe Kevin Federlines (dancers, that is) to general shoot-'em-up maniacs. Look out for offers, such as student nights, 'Lord of the Pins' bowling challenge and cheap midweek drinks.

☺ *Mon–Sun, 10am–12am*

☺ *£2.60 per game (off-peak), £4 (peak)*

Out & About

The Metrodome Waterpark

Queens Road, Barnsley

(01226) 730 060

Terrorship 3000, Space Bullet and Alien Mountain? No, they're not the names of three dodgy 70s B-movies (actually, they probably are, but we don't do film reviews). They're the names of the three amazing white-knuckle slides at the Metrodome. Kids and big kids alike will have a whale of a time. You might have to travel out of Sheffield to experience The Metrodome, but this much fun is worth braving 20 minutes on the old Midland Mainline train for.

☻ *Mon, 9am–8pm; Tue–Fri, 9am–7pm; Sat–Sun, 10am–5pm (school holidays); Mon, 4pm–8pm; Tue–Fri, 4pm–9pm; Sat–Sun, 10am–5pm (term time)*

☻ *£4.95*

The Sheffield Ski Village

Sheffield Ski Village Vale Road, Park Springs

(0114) 276 9459

Legend states that, like Rome, Sheffield is built upon seven hills. So it's no wonder that the city plays host to Europe's largest artificial ski resort. In fact, why don't you try and sneak some skis out with you, as they're bound to come in handy as you explore the rest of the city. (Obviously Itchy does not endorse criminal behaviour of any kind, including theft. Even if the thought of somebody trying to hide a pair of full-sized skis underneath their jumper so they look like a gigantic pair of boobs does make us chuckle).

☻ *Mon–Fri, 10am–10pm; Sat–Sun, 9am–7pm*

☻ *£10.30–£14.60 for 1 hour*

Sheffield United Football Ground

Bramall Lane, Cherry Street

(0870) 787 1960

If you fancy sampling some weekend sport, look no further than Sheffield United Football Club. The Blades' recent relegation should not dampen your enthusiasm. Without Neil Warnock, there's not half as much complaining and excuses. You can also feel a part of history, as Bramall Lane is the oldest major stadium in the world still to be hosting professional football matches. A Saturday afternoon at the football has become an expensive trip out, but at Sheffield United you can often get cheap concession and student tickets, and the food and drink are fairly priced.

☻ *£5–£25*

Laters

You Snooze, You Lose

MISSING OUT ON LATE-NIGHT FUN BECAUSE YOUR GROOVY TRAIN IS STUCK IN LAZY TOWN? WANNA BE A MEMBER OF THE WIDE AWAKE CLUB, BUT YOUR DOZY HEAD FEELS HEAVIER THAN MALLETT'S MALLET? YOU NEED ITCHY'S MINI A-TO-ZED OF WAYS TO STAY AWAKE FOR DAYS…

If you don't want to set foot in the Land of Nod for a whole 24 hours, preparation must begin at breakfast time. If, like us, you like to kick your day off with a Weetabix or two, you'll know that dried-up cereal is one of the stickiest, most viciously viscous substances known to man. Smear a little porridge onto your eyelids and press them up towards your brows. Next, hold your head over the toaster to accelerate the drying process. Result: your peepers will be glued open permanently, or until it rains.

Worrying is a great way to stave off the sandman. Want to stay wired throughout a week-long holiday or festival? Go for an STD test just before things kick off. It'll be an agonising seven days before your results come through, during which time you won't sleep a wink.

Threadworms are known to be more active at night. Pick up your own wriggly-ass infestation by babysitting for your neighbourhood's grubbiest kids, then enjoy hours of sleeplessness courtesy of an intensely itchy bum. It's guaranteed you'll still be up at the – ahem – 'crack' of dawn.

Or, watch that kinky home video you discovered in your ma and pa's camcorder collection. Better than any horror film for making sure you'll never sleep again.

Illustration by Si Clarke

LATE-NIGHT SHOPPING

Does the daily grind mean that to your horror there's no time left for shopping? Well worry no more for **Meadowhall (1 The Oasis, 0114 256 8800)** can feed that money spending bug inside you. Open until 9pm there's plenty of time to get lost at least twice in the maze of aisles and still bag a treat. Alternatively, if it happens to be a Thursday or Friday, you could take a trip to **Crystal Peaks (Eckington Way, 0114 251 0457)**, open until 8pm. Now you'd probably only choose this location if you needed cheaper shops and had a bit of a penchant for teenage mums, but hey, whatever floats your boat.

FAGS AT 4am

You can't fight the craving til morning and have to have nicotine right here right now. It's for your friends too; you don't want to let them face your ciggie-starved wrath. When you can't stop the shaking and twitching get to trusty old **Spar (Division Street, 0114 275 2900)**. The bloomin' place never closes. Not in the town centre though? Then head to the **Ecclesall Mini-market (375 Ecclesall Road, 0114 267 6439)** where there's even a cash machine inside to help fund your habit. Failing that, call in at **Alldays (486 Glossop Road, 0114 267 8440)** and grab a loaf while you're there.

LATE-NIGHT DRINKING

Want a trendy, stylish and generally getting-down-with-your-bad-self kinda night? For some kicking beats in a cool-for-cats atmosphere get yourself to **DQ (Fitzwilliam Street, 0114 201 2653)**. Open 'til 4am if you're the kind that likes to hear the birds singing when you leave. Perhaps cheese is more your thing though, and nowhere's better to coat yourself in it from head to foot than **Flares (2–8 Carver Street, 0114 279 5581)**. Its 3am opening on a Saturday means you can live the John Travolta dream that little bit longer. Alternatively, for a more chilled night **The Harley (334 Glossop Road, 0114 275 2288)** will see you right. Live bands and pub quizzes 'til the early hours, what more could you want?

POST CLUB ACTION

Can't find any early hours action? Well let the rest of Sheffield go to bed and make your own fun and do a big shop at a 24hr supermarket. You can also take advantage of the quiet aisles to have trolley races with your mates. Find an unusual way to get home: try to make it all the way back without touching the pavement, or swap clothes with as many people as possible. It could get interesting. Re-enact your favourite musical and burst into a song and dance routine with your mates, surrounding an unsuspecting bystander and shaking jazz hands at them, bringing that Broadway spirit right into the heart of Sheffield.

FOOD NOW!

Whether you need that post-beer satisfaction of pure stodge or you've just woken up in the early hours and have a sudden urge to eat chicken kebab with cheesy chips, look no further than these lip smacking venues... at **The Devonshire Chippy (105 Devonshire Street, 0114 249 3343)** you'll get the best chip butty you've ever tasted at 3 o'clock in the morning – or indeed at any time of the day or night – and one of those clumsy wooden forks with which to shovel it into your face hole. **Balti King (216 Fulwood Road, 0114 266 6655)** holds the crown in the world of curries, so grab yourself a ruby before passing out with a naan bread stuck to the side of your face. For your typical takeaway, **Elif (529 Ecclesall Road, 0114 266 6876)** will never fail you, and their kebabs actually come on skewers rather than in a soggy pitta bread for that touch of class. So, there you go, no more will you have to attack the mounds of frozen bread, stuck together in the bottom of your freezer, just to avoid going to bed with a stomach emptier than Tom Cruise's hopeful Oscar shelf.

OTHER LATE-NIGHT INDULGENCES

Fancy doing something for the evening which doesn't involve alcohol? How about a bit of innocent frittering away of money then? **Napoleon's Casino (844 Ecclesall Road, 0114 266 1115)** will provide endless hours of blackjack or roulette fun. Or you could exercise that arm of yours with a spot of bowling at **Hollywood Bowl (Valley Centertainment, 0114 244 4333)**. Playing through 'til midnight means you'll miss all those screaming, annoying kids too. If you want something a little more relaxing though, why not sit back and take in a late night film at **Vue (Meadowhall Shopping Centre, 0871 224 0240)**? Just make sure you don't fall asleep in your chair for the cleaners to find you drooling down your shoulder by the end of the movie.

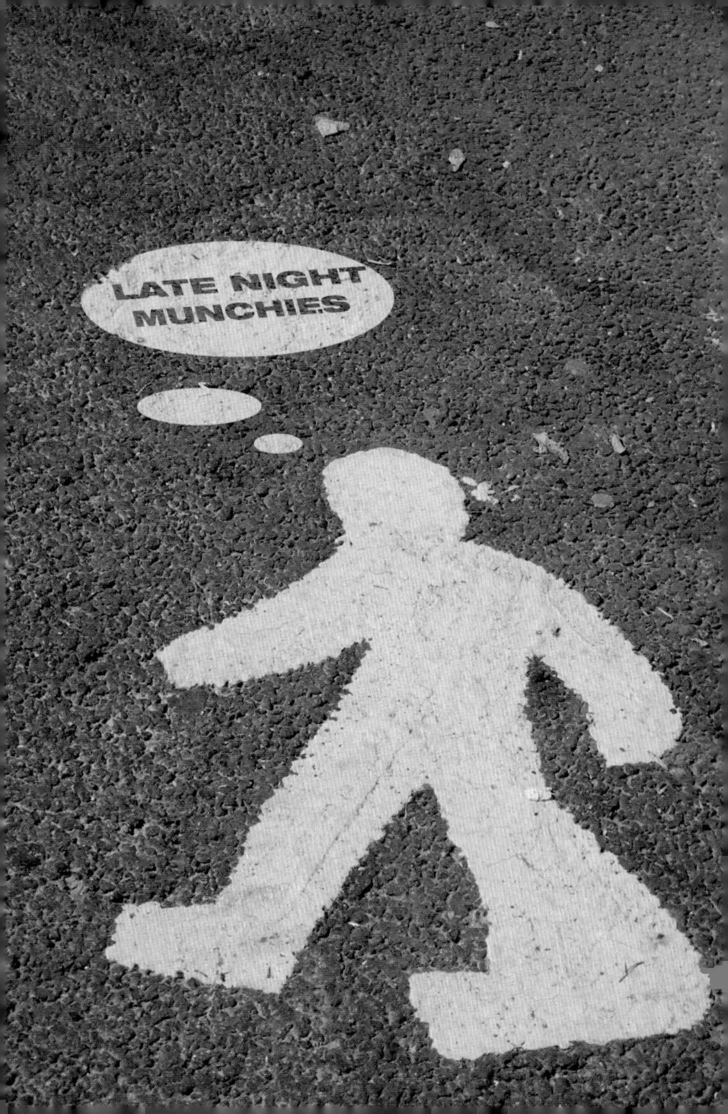
LATE NIGHT
MUNCHIES

Sleep

Sleep

CHEAP

Beauchief Hotel
161 Abbeydale Road South
(0114) 262 0500

Just a hop-skip from the Peak District, the Beauchief has a comfy bed to fall into when all the walking finally catches up with you...

🛏 *From £40 per person with breakfast*

Farfield Inn
376 Neepsend Lane
(0114) 272 8520

A comfy and quaint bed and breakfast situated five minutes from the city centre and a world away from all the unsightly hustle and bustle. For those more concerned with a good sleep than a crazy night out.

🛏 *Standard rate room, £30*

MID-RANGE

City Crash Pad Serviced Apartments
111 West Street
(0114) 201 4321

A bit of a change from your standard hotel room, these are apartment rooms to rent.

🛏 *Studio apartment per night, £45*

The Rutland Hotel
452 Glossop Road
(0114) 266 4411

Located just one mile from the city centre, The Rutland Hotel is the largest private hotel in Sheffield. It's recently undergone a £1 million refurbishment, but retains a good sense of Victorian splendour. Which is nice.

🛏 *Bed and breakfast, from £69.50*

Ibis Hotel
Shude Hill
(0114) 241 9600

Ideally placed in the city centre, for when you come crawling to bed sometime in the wee hours. The supertram is right outside, so if you really can't manage to put one foot in front of the other, you can ride the rails.

€ *From £50 per night*

Premier Travel Inn
Angel Street/Bank Street
(0114) 250 2802

You know what these guys are about; we know what they're about – decent accommodation and not unheard-of prices. A good place to kick off your boots and sleep the day off.

€ *Mon–Thu, from £60; Fri–Sat, £58*

SWANKY

Aston Hall
Worksop Road
(0114) 287 2309

Aston Hall is a scenic paradise for all those who want to say farewell to the urban life without really having to go anywhere.

€ *From £139 with breakfast*

Mercure St Paul's Hotel & Spa Sheffield
119 Norfolk Street
(0114) 278 2000

An über-chic hotel for über-cool people, and you get to look out at the pretty plants of the Winter Gardens situated next door. This place can get expensive though.

€ *Double rooms starting at £75 per night*

If You're **Starting** from Scratch

You'd better get

Itchy

Baltis in Birmingham?,
Cocktails in Cardiff?,
Gigs in Glasgow?

For the best features and
reviews of where to go all
over the UK, log on to:
www.itchycity.co.uk

www.itchycity.co.uk

**Bath/Birmingham/Bristol/Cardiff/Edinburgh
Glasgow/Leeds/Liverpool/London/Manchester
Nottingham/Sheffield**

Useful info

HAIRDRESSERS

Freestylers

547 Ecclesall Road

(0114) 266 9119

'Dey ain't gonna bust no crazy rhymes on your bad self here bro'. Instead you'll get a blooming good haircut. Innit.

◎ *Mon–Fri, 10am–7pm; Sat, 9am–5pm*

Hair Waves

207 School Road

(0114) 266 1690

Make waves in the fashion world. Ok, it's not as glamorous or upmarket as other places but, if it's just a quick trim you're after, you'd be hard pushed to find better.

◎ *Mon–Wed & Fri, 9am–5pm; Thu, 9am–7pm; Sat, 9am–3pm*

The Hairband

625 Ecclesall Road

(0114) 268 5685

You won't need a hairband after coming here. In fact, given the free drinks and lovely staff you won't ever want to leave.

◎ *Mon, 9am–5pm; Tue, 9am–5.30pm; Wed–Fri, 9am–8pm; Sat, 9am–5pm; Sun, 9.30am–4.30pm*

La Coupe Studio

Unit 15, 4 Orchard Square

(0114) 275 0505

It's as though these guys were born with a pair of scissors in their hand; they'll have your barnet looking brand new in no time and you won't want to curl up and die after.

◎ *Mon–Tue, 10am–5pm; Wed–Fri, 10am–7pm; Sat, 9am–5pm; Sun, 11am–4pm*

BEAUTY AND SPA

Mint Nail and Beauty Bar

19 The Arcade, Meadowhall Centre

(0114) 256 9292

This fancy pants nail bar is just the ticket to get yourself feeling in mint condition.

◎ *Mon–Fri, 9am–9pm; Sat, 9am–7pm; Sun, 9am–5pm*

Spa 1877

67 Victoria Street

(0114) 221 1877

Relaxing Turkish baths, without the sweaty bearded woman scrubbing half the skin off your back. You'll come out feeling fresher than a new springtime lamb.

◎ *Mon–Fri, 9.30am–9.30pm; Sat–Sun, 9am–6.30pm*

TRAINS

Midland Mainline
(08457) 125 678
Just don't mention the state of their trains.

National Rail enquiries
(08457) 484 950
All you need to know, pre-platform.

TOURIST INFORMATION

Sheffield Information Centre
12 Norfolk Row
(0114) 221 1900
Not as good as Itchy, but by all means viisit them for the kind of information a tourist needs.
🕑 *Mon–Sat, 9am–5.30pm; Sun, 9am–6pm*

TAXIS

A1 Cars
64a Abbeydale Road
(0114) 250 0555
What is it about bands and Sheff taxi firms?

Central Travel
Vale Road
(0114) 276 7000

R.E.M Travel
59 Compton Street
(0114) 231 2783
Our driver looked a bit like Mr Stipe.

Sheffield Taxi Service Limited
50 Burton Road
(0114) 275 1111

CAR RENTAL

Alamo Rent-A-Car
40 Corporation Street
(0870) 191 6921

WhizzGo Car Share
Cathedral Chambers, Great George Street
(0870) 446 6000

PLANES

Sheffield City Airport
Europa Link
(0114) 201 1998
We don't think BA will be doing flights to Ibiza from there just yet. Settle for a trip to Dublin instead, it's a much better option for the wallet and your carbon footprint.

Useful info

TAKEAWAY CHIPPY

Broomhill Friery

197 Whitham Road

(0114) 266 2802

This little fish and chippy has cult status and is rumoured to be Ainsley Harriot's favourite. No further comment needed.

🕒 *Mon–Sat, 11.30am–11pm*

Two Steps

294 Sharrowvale Road

(0114) 266 5694

Some of the best chips in Sheffield are proud to call this place home. Well, it's been around for donkeys' years, so you'd expect them to be getting it right by now.

🕒 *Mon–Sat, 11.30am–2.30pm & 5pm–10pm; Sun, 5pm–10pm*

TAKEAWAY CURRY

Balti King

216 Fulwood Road

(0114) 266 6655

Check out their menu online. Prices are good and their delivery is fast.

🕒 *Mon–Thu, 12pm–3am; Fri–Sat, 12pm–4am; Sun, 12pm–2am*

The Mogul Room

282 Sharrowvale Road

(0114) 267 9846

A bhuna King among crappy kormas, this classy establishment never ceases to curry favour with the locals. You'll always go back for their delicious baltis.

🕒 *Sun–Thu, 5.30pm–11.30pm; Fri–Sat, 5.30pm–12.30am*

TAKEAWAY CHINESE

Golden Lee

279 London Road

(0114) 258 5890

The only downside to the Golden Lee is that they only deliver within a very small area. Try the chicken and Chinese mushrooms.

🕒 *Mon–Sun, 5pm–11pm*

Wok This Way

394 Fulwood Road

(0114) 230 3008

The food may be no better or no worse than any of the other Chinese takeaways littered about Sheffield's studenty areas but, for us, the name always tips the scales in favour of this place.

🕒 *Mon–Sun, 5pm–11.30pm*

TAKEAWAY PIZZA

Perfect Pizza

294 Prince of Wales Road

(0114) 265 0007

Be warned, once you try pizza perfection, you'll find it hard to resist ordering a fresh, cheesy plate of deliciousness every night.

🕒 *Mon–Sun, 4.30pm–12am*

Pisa Pizza

237 Crookes

(0114) 266 6080

Along with their excellent alliteration skills, this lot are also excellent at cooking up fresh pizzas. Throw in the fact that the meal deals here are cheap as chips and why would you bother eating anywhere else?

🕒 *Mon–Sun, 5pm–1am*

Support

24-hour Locksmith
Andy Locks
(0114) 228 0913

24-hour Electrician
Pickford Power Services
(07930) 673 493

24-hour Plumber
PB Plumbing
(0114) 265 3608

A & E Department
Royal Hallamshire Hospital
(0114) 271 3279

Emergency Dentist
Charles Clifford Dental
Hospital
(0114) 271 7999

Samaritans
(0114) 276 7277

Local Police
South Yorkshire Police
(0114) 220 2020

Family Planning Clinic
Sheffield Contraception
Sexual Health
(0114) 271 6816

Citizens Advice Bureau
(0114) 250 1144

Late Night Pharmacy
Wicker Pharmacy
(0114) 272 7676

Student Welfare/Union
University of Sheffield
Careers Service
(0114) 222 0910

Rape Helpline
SRASACS
(0114) 244 7936

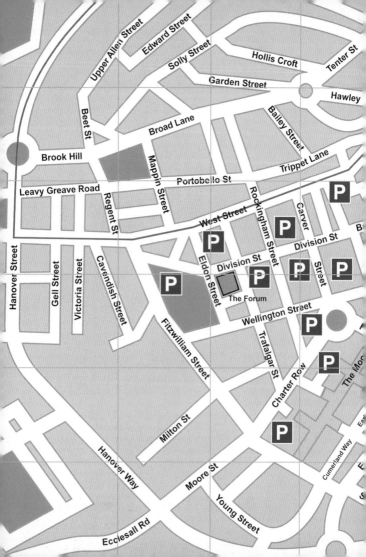

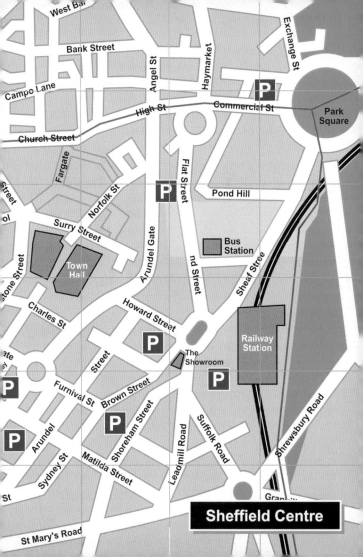

Index